KW-067-477

A2 Business Studies

Contents

Introduction

■ ■ ■

Content Guidance

■ ■ ■

Questions and Answers

Introduction

About this guide

This Student Unit Guide has been written with a single objective in mind: to provide you with the ideal resource for your revision of AQA Unit 4, A2 business studies. After this introductory note on the aims and assessment of A-level business studies, the guide is divided into two sections: Content Guidance and Questions and Answers.

The first section offers concise coverage of Module 4: Marketing and Accounting and Finance, and Module 5: People and Operations Management, which together cover a large amount of material. Students should recognise that Unit 4 assesses both Modules 4 and 5. By necessity, this guide only provides an overview of the key terms and concepts together with an identification of opportunities for you to illustrate the higher-level skills of analysis and evaluation. The scope for linking different topic areas is also shown.

The second section is based upon four case studies following the Unit 4 format exactly. Each case study is followed by two sample answers (a grade A and a lower-quality response) interspersed with examiner comments.

Each Unit 4 case study contains four questions covering Modules 4 and 5 of the specification. Thus, the case study contains one question on each of marketing, accounting and finance, operations management and people and organisations. All of these questions are worth 20 marks, though they may be subdivided into two sections. It is perfectly possible to read the relevant section on, say, marketing and then to attempt the marketing questions from one or more case studies. However, it is recommended that you attempt at least one of these case studies at a single sitting to practise and develop all your examination skills, not least time management. In this case, it will be essential to read all of the Content Guidance section before you start writing.

The aims of the A-level qualification

A-level business studies aims to encourage candidates to:

- develop a critical understanding of organisations, the markets they serve and the process of adding value
- be aware that business behaviour can be studied from the perspectives of a range of stakeholders including customers, managers, creditors, owners/shareholders and employees
- acquire a range of skills, including those involved in decision-making and problem-solving
- be aware of current business structure and practice

A2 Business Studies
UNIT 4

Module 4: Marketing and Accounting and Finance
Module 5: People and Operations Management

Malcolm Surridge

Series Editor: John Wolinski

Philip Allan Updates
Market Place
Deddington
Oxfordshire
OX15 0SE

tel: 01869 338652
fax: 01869 337590
e-mail: sales@philipallan.co.uk
www.philipallan.co.uk

ISBN-13: 978-0-86003-498-8
ISBN-10: 0-86003-498-4

This Guide has been written specifically to support students preparing for the AQA A2 Business Studies Unit 4 examination. The content has been neither approved nor endorsed by AQA and remains the sole responsibility of the author.

Typeset by Good Imprint, West Sussex
Printed by Information Press, Eynsham, Oxford

Assessment

AS and A2 papers are designed to test certain skills. **Every mark that is awarded on an AS or an A2 paper is given for the demonstration of a skill.** The content of the course (the theories, concepts and ideas) exists to provide a framework to allow students to show their skills: recognising the content on its own is not enough to merit high marks.

The following skills are tested:

- **Knowledge and understanding** — recognising and describing business concepts and ideas.
- **Application** — being able to explain or apply your understanding to a variety of business scenarios.
- **Analysis** — developing a line of thought in order to demonstrate its causes, impact or consequences.
- **Evaluation** — making a judgement by weighing up the evidence provided.

The table below shows the marks awarded for skills for A2 Unit 4.

Skill	Marks	Description
Knowledge	16	How well you know definitions, theories and ideas.
Application	21	How well you can explain benefits, problems and calculations.
Analysis	27	How well you develop ideas and relate theory to circumstances.
Evaluation	16	How well you judge the overall significance of the situation.
Total	80	

The skills requirement of a question

There are two guides to the skills requirement of a question. First, its mark allocation gives a rough indication of what is required. In the case of Unit 4 (90 minutes), 84 marks are available (including 4 marks for quality of language). For individual questions worth 20 marks, the mark allocation is approximately as follows:

Up to 4 marks	a definition or description showing **knowledge**
A further 5 marks	an explanation or calculation showing **application**
Another 7 marks	development of an argument in the context of the question showing **analysis**
A final 4 marks	a supported judgement of a situation or proposed action demonstrating **evaluation**

These skills are awarded separately. Therefore, if you write an evaluative response you will not gain all the marks for the lower-level skills automatically. It is important to structure answers carefully to ensure that you demonstrate all the necessary skills. Thus it is a good idea to commence your answers by defining key business terms in the question, as this is an excellent way to earn **knowledge marks.** Relating your answer to the scenario or carrying out calculations will be awarded by **application marks.**

Second, another (and better) guide to the skills requirement of a question is to look at the trigger word (or verb) within the question. **Specific trigger words will be used to show you when you are required to analyse or evaluate.** Examples for A-level business studies include:

Analyse
- 'Analyse...'
- 'Examine...'
- 'Explain why...'
- 'Why might...?'
- 'Use...to explain...'

Evaluate
- 'Evaluate...'
- 'Discuss...'
- 'To what extent...?'
- 'Assess...'
- 'Consider...'
- 'Comment upon...'

Most of the questions on AQA Unit 4 require analysis or evaluation, so these words will be commonplace. However, on each paper it is likely that one part of a question might require lower-level skills, possibly just explanation or application. In such a case, command words other than those listed above will be used and the mark allocation will be quite low.

Students who fail to **analyse** generally do so because they have curtailed their argument. Certain words and phrases serve to provide logical links in an argument. By using them you can demonstrate your ability to analyse. For example, you can use:
- 'and so...'
- 'but in the long run...'
- 'which will mean/lead to...'
- 'because...'

In order to **evaluate**, you need to demonstrate judgement and the ability to reach a reasoned conclusion. The following terms will demonstrate to the examiner that this is your intention:
- 'The most significant...is...because...'
- 'However,...would also need to be considered because...'
- 'The decision may depend upon...'
- 'The probable result is...because...'

Opportunities for evaluation in Modules 4 and 5

The Unit 4 examination covers a great deal of material and places a significant emphasis on evaluation (20% of the marks are awarded for this skill). This means that there are a considerable number of opportunities for evaluation and analysis. Examples of these opportunities are listed at the end of each element of the Content Guidance section.

Revision strategies

Some general pieces of advice for examination preparation are:
- Prepare well in advance.

- Organise your files, ensuring there are no gaps.
- Read different approaches — there is no single right approach to business studies. Experience as many views and methods as possible. Read newspapers and business articles regularly throughout the A-level course.
- When reading an article, try to think of types of question an examiner might ask and how you would answer them. Your Unit 4 case study will be based on a business scenario and wide reading will help to familiarise you with a variety of businesses and circumstances.
- Take notes as you read. These will help to:
  - put the text into your own words, cementing your understanding
  - summarise and emphasise key points
  - focus your attention
  - précis information which could help with future revision
  - boost your morale by showing an end product of your revision sessions
- Develop and use your higher-level skills. Make sure that your revision is not dominated by factual knowledge alone. Check you can explain and analyse the points covered, and try to imagine situations in which evaluation can be applied.
- Practise examination questions. Use the questions in this book (and past papers when available) to improve your technique, making sure you complete all the questions in the time allowed. In the examination you have 90 minutes to read the case study and answer the questions. Allowing 10 minutes for reading, you have 80 minutes to earn 80 marks, so allocate 1 minute to each mark available on the question. So, if the question is worth 12 marks, you should devote 12 minutes to it.
- Maintain your motivation. Reward yourself for achieving targets, but do not get demoralised if you fall behind. If necessary, amend your objectives to a more realistic level.
- Find out the dates and times of your examinations and use this information to prepare a detailed schedule for the study leave/examination period, making sure you build in time for relaxation and sleep.
- Focus on all the areas relevant to Unit 4, as questions covering all the topics comprising Modules 4 and 5 will be included. Do not merely focus on your favourite topics. Your revision is more likely to 'add value' if it improves your understanding of an area you find difficult. Revising a topic you already know is a morale booster, but is it as valuable?
- Top up your memory just before the examination. If there are concepts, formulae or ratios that you find difficult, revisit them just before the examination.
- Adopt your own strategy. Everyone has a different learning style: use one that suits you.

Content
Guidance

This section of the guide outlines the topic areas of Modules 4 and 5, many of which build upon the work completed at AS. These are as follows:

- market analysis
- marketing strategy
- marketing planning
- company accounts
- ratio analysis
- contribution and break-even analysis
- investment decision-making
- communication
- employer–employee relations
- human resource management
- productive efficiency
- controlling operations and facilities

Because of the amount of subject matter covered by Modules 4 and 5, this section only provides an outline of the necessary material.

Key concepts

Key concepts are defined or shown in bold. You should have a business studies dictionary to hand.

Analysis

Under this heading there are suggestions on how topic areas could lend themselves to analysis. During your course and the revision period you should refer to these opportunities. Test and practise your understanding of the varied ways in which a logical argument or line of reasoning can be developed.

Evaluation

Under this heading general opportunities for evaluation are highlighted within particular topic areas.

Marketing

Market analysis and marketing strategy

Asset- and market-led marketing

Asset-led marketing entails a company using its assets as a central part of its marketing, thereby promoting its strengths. A business could use a well-known brand name in this way or employ a major tangible asset it owns as an important aspect of its marketing. Thus the Virgin Group engages in asset-led marketing by using its brand name on all of its products.

Market-led marketing results when businesses consider consumers' needs and the actions of competitors. Such firms continually analyse consumers' needs and ensure that they fulfil them. They are continually alert to changes occurring in the market-place and ready to respond to threats and/or opportunities as they emerge. A market-led firm may benefit by:

- being able to predict market changes more accurately
- being able to launch new products more confidently as the chance of failure is reduced
- being prepared for changes in demand and responding promptly

Analysis of trends

A trend is the underlying pattern of growth or decline within a series of data. Looking at just a few figures may not be helpful. Hence a firm will attempt to establish any trends, e.g. are sales in a particular area rising? This enables the firm to plan production to meet the demands of the market, so helping it to use its resources effectively.

Extrapolation analyses the past performance of a variable such as sales and extends this into the future. Establishing the pattern of historic data will help the business to predict what might happen in the future. If a firm has enjoyed a steady increase in sales over a number of years, the process of extrapolation is likely to forecast a continued steady rise. This is simply done by eye.

Extrapolation
- is easy to carry out as it merely involves extending a trend
- may be inaccurate as it assumes that the future will be similar to the past
- is not suitable for use in environments subject to rapid change

More scientific approaches to establishing trends in a series of data may be used. **Moving averages** are a series of calculations designed to show the underlying trend within a series of data. The use of moving averages should smooth out the impact of random variations in data and longer-term cyclical factors, thus highlighting the trend.

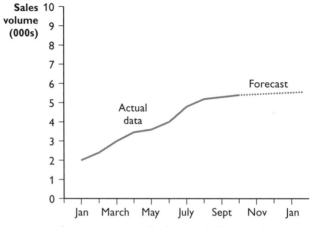

Figure 1 Extrapolation and the trend

By predicting trends, firms are able to forecast future sales. This information is invaluable in helping to plan production and draw up human resource plans, and is the basis of much financial planning.

Correlation is a statistical technique used to establish the extent of the relationship between two variables. Correlation can be an important technique for those involved in marketing.

Correlation
- can show the extent of a relationship (if any) between key variables such as sales and expenditure on promotion
- can be presented on a graph as in Figure 2 (below)
- provides information to assist managers in decision-making

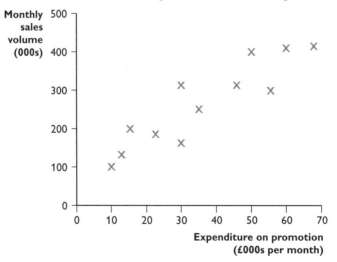

Figure 2 A scatter graph demonstrating close correlation between sales volume and expenditure on promotion

Analysis Consider the reasons why a business might adopt an asset-led or a market-led approach to its marketing. The arguments in favour and against either approach could include:
- the extent to which the business relies upon its assets in trading activities
- the nature of the assets available to a business
- the rate of change in the market

The analysis of trends and correlations can be based on the advantages and disadvantages of different methods. For example:
- relatively simple and quick techniques may be available to most managers
- using less than perfect information may be better than operating on instinct
- historic data may not give a good indication of the future
- it may be preferable to use market research to gain relevant information

Evaluation Look out for indicators of opportunities for evaluation.
- The importance of the approach depends upon the nature of the business — asset-led marketing may be appropriate for a traditional hotel, but not for a clothes manufacturer.
- All statistical techniques depend upon the accuracy of the data — over what period were they collected and what approaches were used?
- Analysis of trends is of less potential value in a rapidly-changing market, since the past will be a less accurate indicator of the future.

Links Market-led and asset-led marketing have obvious links with other topics within marketing, for example market research and promotion. Other links exist in relation to the purchase of fixed assets and also the competitive structure of the market.

Market planning

Marketing decision-making

The marketing model is a structure outlining the process by which marketing decisions can be taken on a scientific basis. This scientific approach is an alternative to managers taking decisions on the basis of hunches or guesses. The marketing model involves a number of stages:
- setting marketing objectives (contributing to corporate objectives)
- gathering data and forming a judgement about marketing actions
- testing the hypotheses
- reviewing the process

This model has been developed from F. W. Taylor's scientific approach to decision-making and is continuous. Reviewing the process may lead to modification of the objectives, the market research (data gathering), or the chosen marketing actions.

Analysis This could consider the pros and cons of taking marketing decisions on a scientific basis. Some pros are:
- it means more data are likely to be considered
- it may involve more people in the decision-making process

But, on the cons side:
- it may be slower because of the degree of research and consultation
- it might lack occasional inspired actions on the basis of hunches

Evaluation It would be appropriate to consider situations where quick decisions are required and scenarios where detailed data may not be available on which to base a decision. The fashion industry, for example, might be an industry in which hunches and guesses could be more usefully deployed.

The size of the business might be an important factor too. Large businesses, dealing with more complex marketing decisions, might have greater need of a more scientific approach.

Links There is a direct link to objectives and strategy as corporate objectives will be a major influence. Close links exist between marketing and production in terms of design, developing prototypes and supplying sufficient products. The human dimension should not be ignored: scientific decision-making requires employees to have the correct skills to take the decision and to deal with the consequences of the decision.

Planning and the marketing mix

This is a development of the marketing mix you will already have covered at AS (combining the four major tools of marketing — price, product, promotion and place — used by a business to influence the behaviour of consumers).

A firm's marketing strategy is designed to assist the firm in achieving its corporate objectives. The strategy itself determines what goods and services are to be offered and in what markets. The role of the marketing mix is to implement the firm's marketing strategy. The mix determines how these products are presented to the customer.

Marketing planning involves developing the tactics necessary to implement the marketing strategy. It involves:
- establishing targets for marketing
- developing the different elements of the mix to make sure they are coordinated
- deciding on a budget for marketing overall and the activities that make it up
- setting targets in terms of time — deciding when marketing objectives should be achieved

Marketing planning assists a business's managers in a variety of ways. For instance:
- The process of planning helps managers to consider all the elements of the plan in detail and to coordinate all activities. It also encourages managers to think strategically.

- Managers can assess the firm's progress by comparing the actual outcomes with the planned outcomes and taking appropriate action if discrepancies appear.
- The plan should provide a sense of direction for managers and assist in determining whether the plan is appropriate to the circumstances.

Marketing budgets

The marketing budget is the amount of money a firm allocates to spend on marketing activities. This money may be used for activities such as advertising and sales promotions. The size of a firm's marketing budget may depend upon:
- the financial position of the firm
- the firm's marketing objectives (challenging objectives may call for greater budgets)
- the size of competitors' budgets

Sales forecasting

A sales forecast states the targets a firm hopes to attain in terms of volume and value of sales. Techniques for sales forecasting include:
- extrapolation of an existing trend
- calculating the trend through moving averages
- using past data to establish causal relationships that will affect sales
- test marketing in order to assess the probable level of sales

Sales forecasts might be inaccurate because:
- a sudden change in tastes and fashions occurs
- competitors' actions and/or responses were unexpected
- the firm conducted inaccurate market research initially
- the market was affected by an unforeseen external factor

Sales forecasts are more likely to be correct when:
- those close to the market (retail managers and sales people, for example) contribute to the formulation of the forecasts
- thorough market research is conducted
- the firm engages in test marketing
- the product is familiar and the market known

> **Analysis** Opportunities for analysis include:
> - arguing the benefits of this type of planning to a particular firm or in a given scenario
> - explaining factors that may cause firms not to plan their marketing
> - examining the implications for a particular firm of a decision to engage in marketing planning
> - examining the relationship between a firm's marketing strategy and its marketing mix
> - explaining why the results of sales forecasting might be inaccurate (or accurate) and the actions businesses might take to improve accuracy
> - arguing the benefits of accurate sales forecasts

Points to consider are:

- The timescale in question — adoption of detailed marketing planning may entail additional short-term costs, with benefits not realised until the long run.
- Does this approach to marketing, with its emphasis on internal communication and consultation, fit with the leadership style, corporate culture etc?
- How rapid is the change in the market? Rapid change may invalidate marketing planning.
- The size of the marketing budget is not all-important — success will also depend upon the skill of the marketing team (and others) and actions of competitors.
- Those factors which are more likely to assist a given firm to achieve accurate sales forecasts.

Links Many links exist from this topic. For example:

- Within marketing, issues such as price elasticity of demand, product portfolio analysis and market research may all be relevant topics.
- Questions of finance may be relevant: liquidity and profitability will influence marketing budgets; sales forecasts will affect cash flow and forecast revenues.
- Marketing planning (and especially sales forecasting) has significant implications for production in terms of range and scale of output.
- Human resource planning will be affected by sales forecasts, as expected sales figures are a vital determinant of the number and types of employees required.

Accounting and finance

Company accounts

Interpreting balance sheets and profit and loss accounts

The balance sheet is a financial statement recording the assets and liabilities of a business at a particular point in time — it is a 'snapshot' of the firm's financial position. By recording assets and liabilities, the balance sheet sets out the ways in which the business has raised its capital and the uses to which this capital has been put.

The profit and loss account records a business's revenues and expenditures, and hence its profit or loss, over a given period of time. When read in conjunction with a business's balance sheet, a profit and loss account allows an analysis to be made of the financial performance of the enterprise. A number of different stakeholders have an interest in a company's published accounts. For example:

- Governments use the information in a private organisations' final accounts for the assessment of taxation, both corporation and value added tax (VAT).
- Shareholders examine the financial information to determine whether or not their business is being properly managed and if their investment is worthwhile.

- Senior managers use company accounts to assist with performance analysis and medium and long-term planning.
- Potential investors compare different organisations to try to decide which offers the best investment opportunity.
- Creditors examine the final accounts of their customers to ascertain their ability to pay.

A range of information can be obtained from reading a company's accounts. Stakeholders can:

- Examine the company's accounts for a number of years, allowing trends in key figures such as revenue and net profit after tax to be assessed.
- Ascertain the balance between capital expenditure (to purchase fixed assets) and revenue expenditure (on day-to-day items such as wages and the purchase of raw materials).
- Assess how the business has raised its capital and the ways in which it has used these funds.
- Make a judgement about the overall value of the business.
- Assess the level of the business's borrowing and whether this poses a risk.
- View and judge a company's revenues, costs and profits.
- Compare this information, which is in a standard format, with that of other companies or of the same firm in previous years.

'Profit' is a term that has a variety of meanings. For example:

- Firms are required to calculate gross profit (before the deduction of overheads) and net profit once all costs are included.
- Profits can be quoted before tax and after tax.
- Retained profits are those remaining once shareholders have received dividends.
- Profit quality varies according to the likelihood of the profit source continuing into the future (e.g. profit from the sale of a fixed asset would be low quality, usually).
- Profit utilisation looks at how the firm uses its profit. Payment of dividends to shareholders may appeal to some shareholders in the short-term, but profit retained in the business will help to fund future growth and profit.

Firms can improve their published accounts through the use of techniques collectively termed 'window dressing'. Instances of this include:

- The sale of fixed assets just before the balance sheet is compiled to improve the business's cash position.
- Bringing forward sales (or delaying expenses) to improve profit figures.
- Overstating the value of certain assets — especially intangible ones such as brands.

Published accounts have a number of limitations. In particular:

- They frequently fail to reveal the full financial picture. For example, a firm incurring heavy costs may be investing for the future.
- The balance sheet only shows the company's position on a particular day and the figures can be manipulated.
- The published accounts give little or no information on the state of the market,

strength of competitors, skills and loyalty of the workforce etc.
- Financial statements convey little information on important issues such as a firm's ethical stance and attitude to its social responsibility.

Analysis A number of opportunities for analysis exist in relation to company accounts, including:
- identifying the main features in a set of accounts, thereby analysing strengths and weaknesses in the company's position
- considering the probable causes and consequences of particular features of a company's accounts
- examining the trend of a company's performance over a period of time or in comparison with another firm
- explaining the actions a business's managers might take to improve the position revealed by the accounts
- comparing elements within the accounts (profits with the level of sales, for example) to give more information on a company's performance

Evaluation Opportunities for evaluation include:
- judging the comparative performance of two companies or the performance of a single business over time
- assessing the importance of financial and non-financial factors in determining a business's overall performance
- demonstrating how firms in different industries and different circumstances might have different features in their balance sheets and profit and loss accounts

Links The financial performance of a business impacts upon nearly every other aspect of a business's activities. For example, it may influence:
- employee morale and productivity, not least if job security is threatened
- the ability of the firm to develop and introduce new products and methods of production

The financial performance of a business may be closely linked to the state of the economy, especially if the products produced have income elastic demand.

Working capital and depreciation

Working capital is a business's current assets less its current liabilities. Working capital is also called net current assets and is shown on a company's balance sheet.

Working capital is important to businesses for a number of reasons:
- Without a surplus of current assets over current liabilities they may be unable to meet their day-to-day expenses.
- It is vital to have sufficient working capital to meet increased costs during periods of expansion — firms that grow without planning for additional working capital are said to be overtrading.
- Having sufficient working capital to be able to meet expenses on time will increase suppliers' confidence and may result in improved terms for trade credit.

To improve its working capital a firm could use one or more of the following techniques:

- Delay payments to creditors by asking for extended periods of trade credit.
- Raise more cash through long-term sources such as share issues or by selling surplus fixed assets.
- Convert short-term liabilities into long-term ones by, for example, changing an overdraft into a long-term loan.

Depreciation is the loss in value of a business *asset* over a period of time. In effect, depreciation allocates the cost of a *fixed asset*, such as a machine or a vehicle, over the lifetime of the asset in question. Although several methods exist for calculating depreciation, the AQA specification only includes the straight-line method, which uses the formula below:

$$\text{annual depreciation} = \frac{\text{initial cost of asset} - \text{residual value}}{\text{expected life of asset in years}}$$

So, a piece of production line equipment with a purchase price of £10,000, a residual (or resale value) of £4,000 and an expected working life of 3 years would be depreciated at £2,000 per annum. This gives the managers and owners of businesses a truer indication of the actual cost of operating the business, rather than including the entire costs of an asset at the time it is purchased.

Analysis Analysis in relation to working capital and depreciation might include:

- considering the nature of the business in relation to working capital (manufacturing businesses normally have a greater requirement for working capital)
- examining the amount of trade credit offered by the business
- analysing the likely cost to the business of raising additional working capital
- explaining factors which might influence a firm's depreciation policies, for example the rate of technological change in the industry or changes in tastes and fashions

Evaluation Themes for evaluation include:

- judging the extent of competitive pressures on the business and its effect on the amount and extent of trade credit offered
- evaluating the benefits and drawbacks to a business of extending its trade credit terms
- assessing the creditworthiness of a particular business and its ability to negotiate (improved) trade credit terms with suppliers
- evaluating the arguments for and against a business seeking to increase or reduce the amount by which it depreciates its assets

Ratio analysis

The focus here is not so much on calculating ratios but rather on interpreting ratios and understanding their implications for business decision-making.

Ratio analysis is a technique for analysing a business's financial performance by comparing one piece of accounting information with another. Ratios can be used to analyse a business's profitability, liquidity and efficiency over a period of time or in comparison with other firms or industry standard figures. Ratios may be used by:
- managers to monitor the performance of the business
- shareholders and potential shareholders to assess likely risk and returns on investments
- suppliers to assess the likelihood of receiving payment and to judge whether to offer credit
- employees to determine the extent of future pay claims
- competitors to benchmark their performances against the firm in question

Ratio analysis is likely to be of greater value to a business if:
- ratios are calculated for a significant period of time
- the results are compared with those of similar firms and industry standard figures
- ratios are considered alongside non-financial information such as that relating to market or economic conditions

Liquidity (including gearing)

Liquidity is the proportion of a business's assets held in a form easily convertible into cash. A firm is liquid if it holds a high proportion of liquid assets such as cash and debtors. Liquidity measures a business's ability to pay its debts on time. Firms seek to hold sufficient liquid assets to ensure that they can fulfil their financial commitments, but not too many since liquid assets earn low returns, if anything. A firm may balance the risk of operating with few liquid assets against the benefits of holding a higher proportion of assets in forms that generate high returns.

Liquidity can be measured using the acid test ratio:

$$\text{acid test ratio} = \frac{\text{liquid assets}}{\text{current liabilities}}$$

where liquid assets are defined as current assets less stock. A 'normal' figure for the acid test ratio might be between 0.6 and 1.1, depending on the type of business.

Gearing is quite often included in the classification of liquidity ratios as this ratio focuses on the long-term financial stability of an organisation. It measures the proportion of capital employed by the business that is provided by long-term lenders as against the proportion that has been invested by the owners. The gearing ratio shows how risky an investment a company is by showing how much of an organisation's capital has been financed by debt:

$$\text{gearing (\%)} = \frac{(\text{long-term liabilities} + \text{preference shares}) \times 100}{\text{total capital employed}}$$

If this ratio is more than 50%, the company is highly geared and may represent a high risk to investors.

Analysis Themes for analysis could include:
- analysing a firm's liquidity and gearing positions from given data
- examining the amount of liquidity required by a particular business — for example retailers may manage with low levels of liquidity
- considering the causes of a firm's poor liquidity position
- arguing how a specific business might improve its financial position with regard to liquidity and gearing

Evaluation Evaluation could centre on the following:
- judging the significance of an acid test result to a particular business
- assessing the 'best' way in which a business might improve its liquidity
- evaluating the risk posed in specific circumstances by a low level of liquidity
- assessing a firm's liquidity and gearing position in the context of the trade cycle and other external influences

Financial efficiency

Financial efficiency may be measured using three ratios.

(1) Asset turnover This ratio measures a business's sales in relation to the assets it uses to generate these sales. The formula to calculate this ratio is:

$$\text{asset turnover} = \frac{\text{sales}}{\text{net assets}}$$

This formula measures the efficiency with which businesses use their assets.

Interpreting the ratio
- An increasing ratio over time generally indicates that the firm is operating with greater efficiency.
- A fall in the ratio can be caused by a decline in sales or an increase in assets employed.
- The results of asset turnover ratios vary enormously. A supermarket may have a high figure as it has relatively few assets in relation to sales. An engineering firm is likely to have a much lower ratio because it requires many more assets.

(2) Stock turnover This ratio measures the number of times in 1 year that a business turns over its stock of goods for sale. It is given by the formula:

$$\text{stock turnover} = \frac{\text{cost of goods sold}}{\text{average stock}}$$

$$\text{where average stock} = \frac{(\text{opening stock} + \text{closing stock})}{2}$$

The result is expressed as however many **times** in 1 year a business turns over its stock of goods for sale.

Interpreting the ratio
- This ratio can only really be interpreted with knowledge of the industry in which the firm operates.
- A greengrocer is likely to turn over stock virtually every day, as goods have to be fresh. Therefore, we would expect to see a result for stock turnover of approximately 250 to 300 times per year.
- A second-hand car sales business would possibly expect to turn over its entire stock of cars and replace them with new ones about once every 2 months. Therefore, we would see a result of 6 times per year.

It is possible to convert this ratio from showing the number of times an organisation turns over stock to showing the average number of days stock is held by using the formula:

$$\text{stock turnover} = \frac{\text{average stock} \times 365}{\text{cost of goods sold}}$$

The result is expressed as **days**.

(3) Debtors' days ratio This ratio shows how long, on average, it takes a company to collect debts owed by customers. Customers who are granted credit are called debtors. The formula for this ratio is:

$$\text{debtor collection period} = \frac{\text{debtors} \times 365}{\text{credit sales}}$$

The result is expressed as **days**.

Interpreting this ratio
- Different industries allow different amounts of time for debtors to settle invoices. Standard credit terms are usually for 30, 60, 90 and 120 days.
- The debt collection period figure should therefore be compared against the official number of days the organisation allows for settlement.
- For this ratio, the shorter the debt collection period the better.

Analysis Issues for analysis in this aspect of the specification will include the following:
- calculating and interpreting the results of financial efficiency ratios
- examining ways in which a firm might improve its financial efficiency
- considering the drawbacks to firms of taking action to improve their financial ratios, e.g. holding less stock may result in dissatisfied customers
- analysing the advantages to be derived from a firm drawing up aged stock and aged debtor analyses

Evaluation Important themes might include:
- evaluating the results in comparison with previous time periods or against other firms' results
- assessing the importance of the results of financial efficiency ratios against non-financial data in taking business decisions

- making some judgements regarding the overall benefits to be gained from a particular business attempting to improve its financial ratios

Profitability ratios

For many businesses in the private sector, profit is an important measure of success. Profit can be measured using several ratios.

(1) Gross profit margin This ratio examines the relationship between the profits made on trading activities only (gross profit) against the level of turnover/sales made. It is given by the formula:

$$\text{gross profit margin} = \frac{\text{gross profit} \times 100}{\text{sales}}$$

The results are expressed as a **percentage.**

Higher gross profit margins are generally preferred. However, the level of gross profit margin made will vary considerably between different markets. For example, the amount of gross profit percentage made on consumer durables, such as televisions, is far higher than that made on food items. Results must be considered in the context of the industry in which the firm operates.

(2) Net profit margin This ratio measures the relationship between the net profit (profit made after all other expenses have been deducted) and the level of turnover or sales made. It is given by the formula:

$$\text{net profit margin} = \frac{\text{net profit} \times 100}{\text{sales}}$$

The results are expressed as a **percentage.**

A higher percentage result is favoured. This ratio establishes whether the firm has been efficient in controlling its expenses.

(3) Return on capital employed (ROCE) This is an important ratio — also called the 'primary ratio'. It measures the efficiency of the business in using its capital to generate profits and is given by the formula:

$$\text{ROCE} = \frac{\text{net profit before tax and interest} \times 100}{\text{total capital employed}}$$

The results are expressed as a **percentage**.

The higher the figure is for ROCE, the better. To assess the ROCE figure for a firm, it should be compared with:

- the business's ROCE figures for previous years
- the ROCE for other companies
- the current rate of interest
- the national average ROCE (currently 13.5%)

Analysis The following could be appropriate lines of analysis:
- calculating and interpreting the results of profitability ratios
- examining ways in which a firm might improve its profitability
- considering the drawbacks to firms of taking action to improve their profitability, e.g. reducing costs by using less expensive materials

Evaluation Important themes for evaluation include the following:
- judging the most effective way in which a firm might boost its profitability
- assessing the importance of profitability to a given business
- evaluating the importance of profitability to different stakeholders in a business
- assessing the extent to which profitability measures the success of a business

Shareholders' ratios

Shareholders are mainly concerned with assessing their expected returns from investing in a particular company.

(1) Dividend per share (DPS) This ratio is the total dividend declared by a company divided by the number of shares the business has issued. It is given by the formula:

$$\text{dividend per share} = \frac{\text{total dividends}}{\text{number of issued shares}}$$

The results of this ratio are expressed as a number of **pence per share** and a higher figure is generally favoured, although some shareholders may prefer a lower DPS if greater returns and a rising share price occur in the future, because the firm is retaining the profit.

(2) Dividend yield This is the dividend per share (for the entire year) expressed as a percentage of the market price of the share. It is given by the formula:

$$\text{dividend yield} = \frac{\text{dividend per share} \times 100}{\text{market share price}}$$

This ratio is also expressed as a **percentage** and shareholders prefer higher figures, preferably exceeding the rate of interest.

Analysis The following could be appropriate lines of analysis:
- calculating and interpreting the results of shareholders' ratios
- examining ways in which a firm might improve its performance for shareholders
- considering the drawbacks to firms of taking action on behalf of shareholders, e.g. declaring a greater dividend to boost DPS might have long-term implications for the company

Evaluation Important themes for evaluation include the following:
- judging the most effective way in which a firm might enhance its image in shareholders' eyes

- assessing the importance of shareholders (against other stakeholders) to a given business
- evaluating the importance of the results of shareholder ratios within a business

Links (for the whole section on ratios) Possible links to other areas include:
- the firm's product portfolio
- the state of the economy – especially the trade cycle
- the management style and human resource plans of the business
- the business's corporate objectives

Contribution and break-even analysis

Contribution can be defined as the difference between sales revenue and variable costs of production.

Contribution has strengths and weaknesses when used as a basis for decision-making.

Strengths	Weaknesses
• Managers in multi-product firms are assisted in making decisions by giving an overview of the entire business.	• Pricing decisions based on contribution do not take market conditions into account.
• The need for arbitrary division of fixed costs is avoided.	• Some costs are difficult to classify as fixed or variable.
• Contribution can provide a flexible basis for pricing decisions.	• In the longer-term, fixed costs can change, thus invalidating earlier decisions based on contribution.

Contribution is an important element in break-even analysis. Break-even is that level of output at which the revenue earned by a firm (or one of its products) is equal to total costs of production.

Break-even analysis is used by firms to guide them in making decisions about:
- whether to start trading
- whether to produce a new product
- the likely profits (or losses) resulting from forecast sales

However, break-even can deal with more complex circumstances including:
- analysing the impact of changing variables (alterations in costs or prices, for example) on the profitability of the business
- deciding whether to accept an order for products at prices different from those normally charged

Change in variable	Impact on break-even output	Other effects
Rise in variable costs	Greater output is necessary to break even.	Due to rise in costs, greater revenues (and so more customers and sales) are necessary to break even.
Fall in variable costs	Smaller output is required to break even.	Each sale incurs lower costs so that a smaller number of customers is needed to cover costs.
Rise in fixed costs	Greater output is required to break even.	Business incurs greater costs before earning any revenue, so more sales will be required to cover cost and break even.
Fall in fixed costs	Smaller output is required to break even.	The business's overall costs are lower and hence fewer sales will be required to break even.
Rise in selling price	Break-even is achieved at a lower level of output.	Each sale will provide the business with greater revenue, whilst costs are unaltered. Hence fewer sales will be necessary to break even.
Fall in selling price	Break-even is reached at a higher level of output.	Every sale will earn the business less revenue so, as costs are unchanged, more sales will be required to earn sufficient revenue to break even.

Special order decisions occur when a business has to decide whether or not to accept orders at a price different from that normally charged. A firm is likely to accept an order for a lower than usual price if:
- the price exceeds the variable cost of production
- the business has sufficient spare capacity to meet the order
- the products will not be resold, undercutting the firm's normal selling price
- accepting the order might result in other benefits — for example the possibility of breaking into a new market

Analysis This area lends itself to analysis based on taking decisions using price and cost data. Thus students may be asked to analyse:
- the effects of changes in price upon break-even output and/or profitability
- the impact of changing fixed or variable costs on break-even output and/or profitability
- whether a firm should accept an order at other than the normal selling price

Evaluation This is likely to centre upon making overall judgements concerning future courses of action for a business combining financial and non-financial information. More specifically students may evaluate by:
- considering the relative importance of financial and non-financial factors in reaching a decision
- assessing the overall value of decision-making techniques based upon contribution and break-even to a firm in specific circumstances

Links Possible links to other areas include:
- the impact of competitors' actions (and market conditions generally) on sales, prices and break-even
- price elasticity of demand measuring the effect of price changes on anticipated sales
- production and capacity — whether the firm can increase output without incurring additional overheads
- the firms' objectives which may affect decisions on low price orders — acceptance is more likely if growth is the primary objective

Investment decision-making

It is important to appreciate that the process of investment involves risk in all circumstances: even the 'safest' investment is not risk-free. Firms use a series of techniques to forecast costs and likely returns, and to judge these figures taking into account non-financial factors and, of course, the degree of risk involved.

Firms can forecast future earnings arising from an investment with more certainty if:
- the market is stable and sales forecasting is relatively straightforward
- competitors' reactions are predictable
- high-quality data (for example on consumers' tastes) are available
- the costs of acquiring relevant data are not too great
- the forecasts do not extend too far into the future
- the economic environment is relatively stable

There are three techniques of investment appraisal in the AQA specification.
(1) Payback This technique evaluates individual investment projects in terms of the time taken to recover the original outlay. In the example below, payback in project A is 3 years and in project B is 2 years.

	Cashflows	
	Project A (£)	Project B (£)
Initial investment	(25,000)	(10,000)
Cash flow year 1	8,000	6,000
Cash flow year 2	8,000	4,000
Cash flow year 3	9,000	2,000
Cash flow year 4	9,000	1,000

(2) The average rate of return This technique assesses the worth of an investment by calculating the yearly percentage return on the sum invested. It uses the formula:

$$\text{ARR} = \frac{\text{average annual profit} \times 100}{\text{initial investment}}$$

This is expressed as a **percentage.**

The average rate of return allows managers to compare alternative investments as well as to contrast the percentage rate of return with that available from investing in financial institutions. The table below shows the average rate of return for an investment in an asset expected to last for 6 years.

Total income from investment	Initial cost of investment	Net profit from investment	Annual average profit (over 6 years)	Average rate of return
£220,000	£100,000	£120,000	£20,000	20%

(3) Net present value (NPV) This uses the technique of discounted cash flow to convert earnings from an investment into their present values: that is the current worth of money at some time in the future. These present values are then added up and the cost of the investment subtracted from the total. What remains is the net present value. NPV must be positive for the investment to be worthwhile. If more than a single investment project is under consideration, the one with the highest NPV will be chosen if the decision is made on financial grounds alone.

NPV uses the rate of interest to convert future earnings into current values. This process, known as discounting, is the reverse of the process of adding compound interest as in the case of a savings account.

The table below highlights the advantages and disadvantages of the three techniques of investment appraisal.

Method of investment appraisal	Advantages	Disadvantages
Payback	Easy to calculate. Simple to understand. Relevant to firms with limited funds who want a quick return.	Ignores timing of payments. Excludes income received after payback. Does not calculate profit.
Average rate of return	Measures the profit achieved on projects. Allows easy comparison with returns on financial investments (bank accounts, for example).	Ignores the timing of the payments. Calculates average profits — they may fluctuate wildly during the project.
Net present value	Makes an allowance for the opportunity cost of investing. Takes into account cash inflows and outflows for the duration of the investment.	Choosing the discount rate is difficult — especially for long-term projects. A complex method to calculate and easily misunderstood.

A number of non-financial factors are likely to affect investment decisions. These include the following:

- The business's objectives. Firms seeking to expand and increase market share may be more willing to invest in projects with a high degree of risk.
- The image of the business. Firms such as Virgin, who seek to appeal to the younger element of the population, are more likely to invest in projects that will enhance this image.
- Industrial relations. Major investments frequently have significant implications for the workforce — redundancies, retraining and redeployment are examples.
- The amount of risk the business is willing to accept. This will depend upon a number of factors, not least the attitudes of the management team.

Analysis Themes for analysis could include the following:
- calculating and interpreting data using one or more of the investment appraisal techniques
- examining the implications of the results of using investment appraisal techniques
- examining the advantages and disadvantages of each of the techniques in relation to a specific context
- analysing non-financial factors that might affect investment decisions

Evaluation This could include:
- making a judgement regarding the applicability of certain techniques of investment appraisal in given circumstances
- evaluating the relative importance of financial and non-financial factors in reaching decisions regarding investment projects
- assessing investment decisions in the context of scenarios and a range of financial and non-financial factors

Links Investment decisions relate to many other areas of the specification. These include:
- Human resource planning — what are the human implications of investment decisions?
- Marketing — does a demand exist for the products that might be produced as a result of the investment?
- The economic environment — how might slump, boom or other economic factors influence the forecasted cash flows arising from the investment projects?

People in organisations

Communication

Communication is the process of exchanging information or ideas between two or more parties. Effective communication offers businesses a number of benefits:

- Successful communication makes it easier to implement change — an important issue in a business environment subject to rapid and continual change.
- It encourages and develops commitment to the business from employees at all levels of the organisation.
- Effective communication helps to ensure that the business is coordinated and that all employees pursue the same corporate objectives.

Poor communication has a number of causes:

- Managers fail to recognise the problem. They may think that symptoms of poor communication (such as poor industrial relations and low levels of motivation) have other causes.
- Leadership styles may discourage effective two-way communication. Some leaders operate an autocratic leadership style within a traditional organisational structure.
- Mergers and take-overs create larger and more complex businesses, increasing the need for information whilst making its transmission more difficult.
- Extending the role and authority of employees creates a greater need for communication, as well as new channels. Techniques such as empowerment and kaizen groups are examples of such developments.

Larger businesses (and especially multinationals) are more likely to experience problems with communications. Inadequate understanding of corporate objectives or different languages, cultures and time zones all make effective communication more difficult. Large firms may place great reliance on technological communication and permit insufficient face-to-face contact.

In a larger business with many intermediaries (a hierarchical structure) the meaning of a message may become distorted, or the communication delayed. In decentralised and delayered organisations the distances involved or the large span of control will add to communication difficulties.

Communication problems, even in large organisations, can be resolved in a number of different ways if managers are prepared to:

- train employees in communication skills
- avoid the danger of generating too much information
- recognise that cultural and linguistic differences exist
- review the leadership style in use and the structure of the organisation
- ensure that corporate objectives are understood by all employees

Analysis This could include:

- examining the possible cause of communication problems for a specific firm
- considering communication problems in relation to particular issues such as leadership styles, techniques of motivation and similar factors
- analysing possible cures for communication problems for specific scenarios
- examining the links that might exist between communication and motivation

Evaluation Opportunities for evaluation in the area include:

- making a judgement as to the most likely cause of communication difficulties in a specific situation
- proposing and justifying a solution for communications difficulties in particular circumstances
- assessing the importance of effective communication in given circumstances

Links Communication links to almost every area of the specification covered by Unit 4: it is a genuinely integrative theme. Examples include:

- production techniques such as lean production and empowerment
- marketing, e.g. market research and promotional activities
- organisational decision-making

Employer–employee relations

Employer–employee relations describe the attitudes of management and employee representatives towards each other. The main elements of employer–employee relations include:

- negotiations about pay and working conditions
- communications between management and employees
- employee participation in management decisions
- policies for improving cooperation between management and employees
- a general approach designed to minimise conflict between the two parties

Types of bargaining and flexible workforces

Individual bargaining takes place when a single employee negotiates his or her own pay and working conditions with management representatives. This has become more common as the role of collective bargaining has declined. The use of collective bargaining in the UK has declined for a number of reasons:

- Trade union membership in the UK has declined over the last 20 years, allowing businesses to abandon collective bargaining.
- Governments have passed legislation designed to allow labour markets to operate more freely, thereby discouraging collective agreements.
- Governments have implemented legislation granting basic protection to employees (from unfair dismissal, from sexual and racial discrimination in employment), meaning that less reliance is placed on the outcome of collective bargaining.
- Employers have introduced strategies (e.g. teamworking) that emphasise and

reward individuals and teams and reduce reliance on the outcomes of collective bargaining.

Many firms in the UK have developed more flexible workforces, leading to a change in employment patterns. The workforce has exhibited the following trends in recent years:
- Increasing numbers of part-time workers — over 7 million by 2001.
- More temporary workers (those on temporary contracts) — the number approached 2 million by 2001.
- Greater use of contractors and consultants providing specialist skills at minimum cost to organisations.
- Declining numbers of permanent full-time employees since the 1980s.

Flexible workforces	
Advantages	**Disadvantages**
• Firms can more easily meet fluctuations in demand. • It is simpler to cover for absent staff. • Wage costs may be reduced. • Firms can meet the demand for highly specialised skills relatively cheaply. • Firms are able to respond rapidly to changing circumstances.	• Communication problems may occur if employees are used irregularly. • It makes systems such as empowerment and teamworking difficult to implement. • Lack of security may detract from employee motivation and morale. • It may result in a higher turnover of labour.

Analysis Lines for analysis include:
- examining the benefits to a firm from adopting individual bargaining
- analysing the costs associated with developing a more flexible workforce
- considering the preparations that may be necessary prior to using a flexible workforce

Evaluation Possible themes for evaluation include the following:
- assessing the balance between benefits and drawbacks of introducing flexible workforces
- judging the case for a business implementing individual bargaining amongst its employees
- evaluating the importance of good employer–employee relations in contributing to the success of a business

Employee participation and industrial democracy

Industrial democracy and employee participation have similar meanings. Both refer to ways in which employees may play a role in the decision-making process of a business. This area is underpinned by the writings of theorists such as Elton Mayo, Abraham Maslow and Frederick Herzberg.

Industrial democracy and employee participation can take a number of forms:
- **Quality circles** — groups of workers who meet regularly to identify methods of improving all aspects of the quality of their products.

- **Works councils** — meetings in which workers and management discuss issues such as working conditions, pay and training.
- **Employee shareholders** — offering workers the chance to have a stake (and possibly a say) in the company through the sale of shares.
- **Autonomous work groups** — teams of employees who are given a high level of control over their working lives as a result of a high degree of delegation.
- **Teamworking** — whereby firms break down the production process into large units of work and give groups of employees control over these processes.

Industrial democracy and employee participation offer a number of advantages:
- They offer the possibility of improved motivation and enhanced productivity and performance.
- They may lessen the possibility of conflict and industrial disputes because employees feel they have a role in decision-making.
- Teamworking allows employers to make the most use of all the talents of their employees.
- Teamworking might reduce management costs (as it is often associated with delayering), assisting in improving productivity.

Analysis Possible lines of analysis include:
- explaining the benefits of industrial democracy and employee participation in terms of motivational theory
- analysing the factors that might influence a business when taking decisions regarding the implementation of industrial democracy and employee participation
- examining the advantages and disadvantages that might result from teamworking and similar techniques

Evaluation Opportunities for evaluation include:
- assessing the extent to which industrial democracy and employee participation are real (as opposed to being an exercise in public relations)
- evaluating the case for and against introducing some degree of industrial democracy or employee participation into a specific business

Trade union law

Trade unions are organisations of workers established to protect and improve the economic position and working conditions of their members. Most trade unions in the UK have similar objectives. These include:
- engaging in collective bargaining to provide their members with the highest possible rates of pay
- achieving safe and secure working conditions
- attaining job security, although this is difficult to fulfil in the light of pressures such as the increasing use of technology in the workplace
- participating in workplace decision-making through collective bargaining or by having representatives on works councils and other employer–employee committees

Trade unions achieve their objectives by carrying out a range of functions to the benefit of their members, including:
- protecting members' interests over issues such as discrimination, unfair dismissal and health and safety matters
- negotiating pay and conditions for their members through collective bargaining
- providing members with a range of personal services (including legal advice, insurance, education, training and financial advice)

Trade union power has declined for the following reasons:
- Conservative governments during the 1980s and early 1990s passed a series of Acts of Parliament gradually limiting the power and influence of trade unions.
- The decline of traditional industries, such as mining, engineering and car manufacture, resulted in the loss of thousands of union members.
- Many foreign businesses locating in the UK have been less welcoming to trade unions.

An **industrial dispute** is a disagreement between an employer and employees (or their trade union representatives) over a range of matters, e.g. pay and working conditions.

These can be resolved in a number of ways:
- **by arbitration** — the parties agree to an arbitrator being appointed, whose decision is in some circumstances legally binding on both parties
- **by conciliation** — a neutral third party attempts to resolve the dispute

Techniques used to avoid industrial disputes include single-union and no-strike agreements. These reduce the possibility of industrial disputes by:
- making industrial relations less confrontational
- improving communication between employer and employees
- focusing employee action on resolving the dispute rather than taking industrial action
- removing the likelihood of inter-union disputes and making the process of negotiation more straightforward

> **Analysis** Themes for analysis include the following:
> - the implications for business of a decline in trade union influence
> - analysing the advantages and disadvantages to a business of recognising a trade union
> - the benefits to a firm resulting from the adoption of a single-union or no-strike agreement
> - examining the ways in which an industrial dispute might be resolved

> **Evaluation** Opportunities for evaluation in this area include:
> - judging the benefits against the drawbacks of trade union recognition for a particular firm
> - assessing the overall case for regulating employer–employee relations through adopting single-union agreements, no-strike deals or binding arbitration

Employment law

The focus of the study of labour law should be on the effects on businesses (and their probable responses) rather than the detail of the legislation.

Employment law can be divided into two distinct elements:
- **individual labour law**, which refers to the rights and obligations of individual employees
- **collective labour laws**, which apply to the operation of industrial relations and collective bargaining, as well as the activities of trade unions.

Much of the UK labour legislation has been strengthened and extended by EU laws.

Individual labour law includes the following:
- **The Equal Pay Act, 1970** This act rules that both sexes should be treated equally in all matters relating to employment.
- **Sex Discrimination Act, 1975** This act makes discrimination on the grounds of sex or marital status illegal in recruitment, promotion, training and dismissal.
- **The Race Relations Act, 1976** This legislation makes it illegal to discriminate in relation to employment, against men or women on the grounds of sex, marital status, colour, race, nationality or ethnic origin.
- **The Disability Discrimination Act, 1995** Employers who treat a disabled person less favourably than others without proper reason are deemed to be behaving illegally under this act.
- **Working Time Regulations, 1998** This European Union legislation (hence the term regulation) sets a voluntary limit on the hours that employees could be required to work each week (48 hours).

There are a number of pieces of collective labour legislation, including:
- **Employment Act, 1980** Under this act employers are no longer obliged to negotiate with unions.
- **Employment Act, 1982** This act makes trade unions liable for damages if the union supports illegal industrial action.
- **Trade Union Act, 1984** This legislation makes a secret ballot of employees a legal requirement before industrial action becomes lawful.
- **Employment Act, 1990** Closed shops are outlawed by this piece of legislation.
- **Trade Union Reform and Employment Rights Act 1993** Unions are required to give employers a minimum of 7 days' notice before taking official industrial action.
- **Minimum Wage Act, 1998** This legislation established a general minimum hourly wage rate (£3.70 an hour in 2000).
- **Employment Relations Act, 2000** Under this act a trade union with a membership exceeding 50% of the employees in any particular business can demand the right to introduce collective bargaining.

Analysis This is mainly a descriptive area of the specification, but two main opportunities for analysis do exist. These are:

- examining the implications (both in terms of opportunities and constraints) for businesses of employment legislation
- considering the possible responses of businesses to newly-enacted employment legislation

Evaluation This would centre on the overall impact of legislation on a particular business or the appropriateness of a particular response to new employment laws in given circumstances.

Links These include:
- A range of matters relating to employer–employee relations affects motivation.
- Methods of production and the degree of difficulty in implementing change are affected by agreements in relation to trade unions.
- Productivity and international competitiveness are likely to be influenced by the recognition of trade unions and the extent of any industrial democracy.
- A business's corporate image may influence its attitudes to employer–employee issues.

Human resource management

Human resource management (HRM) is the strategic process of making the most efficient use of an organisation's employees. HRM views activities relating to the workforce as integrated and vital in helping the organisation to achieve its corporate objectives. Policies relating to recruitment, pay and appraisal should be formulated as part of a coordinated human resource strategy.

Firms have adopted HRM (as opposed to continuing with personnel management) for the following reasons:
- the perceived success of other firms (notably the Japanese) resulting in part from the use of HRM
- flatter organisational structures require a range of managers to take responsibility for looking after employees as part of a coordinated approach
- people are a vital resource for modern businesses, and planning their use should be part of strategic management if a business is to compete in global markets

Workforce planning is one of the central activities of human resource management. Workforce planning entails:
- examining the corporate objectives of the business
- making a judgement about the size and nature of the workforce required over the next few years
- comparing this with the business's current workforce
- deciding upon the necessary policies (recruitment, training, redeployment and redundancy) to match the current workforce to the desired one

A number of factors influence managers when constructing workforce plans:
- Managers must consider the business's corporate plans that state and explain the organisation's overall objectives.

- They must look carefully at the business's marketing and production objectives. These will influence the number and type of employees required in the foreseeable future.
- The financial position of the business is also crucial. Many activities (e.g. training) associated with HRM are expensive and businesses have to operate within tight budgets.
- The state of the market and the economy has to be taken into account too. This is likely to affect the demand for the firm's products and so its need for workers, and the availability and cost of labour.

It is possible to assess the performance of a workforce by using a number of measures.

(1) Labour productivity

$$\text{labour productivity} = \frac{\text{output per period}}{\text{number of employees at work}}$$

(2) Absenteeism (%)

$$\text{absenteeism} = \frac{\text{number of staff absent (on 1 day)} \times 100}{\text{total number of staff}}$$

(3) Labour turnover (%)

$$\text{labour turnover} = \frac{\text{number of staff leaving during the year} \times 100}{\text{average number of staff}}$$

(4) Health and safety (%)

$$\text{health and safety} = \frac{\text{number of working days lost per annum for health and safety reasons} \times 100}{\text{total number of possible working days}}$$

Managers need to measure employee performance to assess the efficiency (and competitiveness) of the workforce. In service firms (where labour costs are a high proportion of total costs) this can be a particularly important factor.

Firms can use financial incentives in order to meet HRM objectives. Piecework, performance-related pay, profit sharing, share ownership and fringe benefits can enhance a salary and be used to achieve greater productivity. They can reduce absenteeism and labour turnover, and encourage employees to adopt new methods or training.

Analysis Opportunities for analysis include the following:
- considering the advantages a business might derive from the process of HRM
- examining the factors that might influence a business whilst engaging in workforce planning
- calculating and interpreting a range of measurements of personnel effectiveness

- examining the factors that might lead to particular results when measuring personnel effectiveness

Evaluation Opportunities for evaluation include:
- assessing the importance of measures of personnel effectiveness in an overall judgement of the performance of a business
- evaluating the case for and against a business adopting HRM — or a particular type of HRM
- making judgements on how an organisation might improve the performance of its workforce
- judging whether HRM is intended to develop or control a particular workforce

Links HRM has links with a number of other areas of the specification. These include:
- Leadership styles — these may affect the type of HRM that is operated.
- Market conditions — actions of competitors and trends in demand will influence a business in its workforce planning.
- Production techniques — changes in techniques (e.g. the adoption of lean production methods) frequently have important implications for HRM.
- The budget-setting process and the development of the workforce are interrelated as recruitment, redundancy and training all involve significant expenditure.

Operations management

Productive efficiency

Productive efficiency is a measure of the success with which a firm turns its inputs into outputs. The more efficient a firm is, the more output it generates with its inputs or the fewer inputs it uses to achieve a given level of output. This section builds directly upon the work completed as part of operations management at AS.

Research and development

Research and development (R&D) is the scientific investigation necessary to discover new products and the process of bringing these products onto the market. The aim of R&D is to develop:
- products which have a unique selling point, allowing a business to differentiate itself from the competition and earn higher profit margins
- better quality products which meet customer needs more successfully
- more efficient ways of producing to reduce the cost per unit

Businesses can gain many advantages from engaging in research and development.

These can include:

- gaining a competitive advantage, perhaps as a result of a more advanced product or a reputation for innovation
- benefiting from a reputation for producing well-designed, high-quality products
- enabling a business to cope with products with short life cycles by producing new products or extending the lives of existing ones
- enabling a business to meet consumers' needs (as identified through market research)

R&D is more likely to be successful if the following criteria are met:

- It is started promptly, i.e. before current products reach the decline stage of their life cycles.
- The results of R&D are protected through the use of copyrights and patents as appropriate.
- Careful attention is given to developing new ideas in such a way that they are attractive to consumers.
- The culture of the business is geared to R&D by, for example, promoting initiative amongst employees at all levels within the organisation.
- The R&D activities are an integral part of the firm's strategy, assisting it in reaching its corporate objectives.

Analysis Opportunities for analysis exist in the following areas:

- analysing the advantages and disadvantages that might result from a particular firm investing in R&D
- examining the factors that might influence a firm in planning its R&D programme
- exploring how R&D might be used by a firm to gain a competitive advantage

Evaluation Opportunities exist for evaluation in a number of areas with regard to R&D, including:

- judging the case for and against a business investing heavily in R&D
- evaluating factors that may result in a programme of R&D proving successful
- assessing the importance of R&D to an organisation's success

Critical path analysis (CPA)

CPA is one type of network analysis. It is a method of calculating and illustrating how complex projects can be completed as quickly as possible. CPA shows the:

- sequence in which the tasks must be undertaken
- length of time taken by each task
- earliest time at which each stage can commence

A CPA network consists of two elements:

- **Activities** This is part of a project requiring time and the firm's resources. The arrows (running from left to right) show the sequence of the tasks.
- **Nodes** These are the start or finish of an activity and are represented by circles. Each node is numbered (in the left-hand segment) and the 'earliest start time' (EST) and 'latest finish time' (LFT) are also stated.

Figure 3 shows an extract from a typical network.

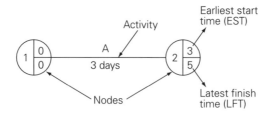

Figure 3 Activities and nodes in critical path analysis

The earliest start times (EST) show the earliest times at which subsequent activities can be commenced. The EST on the final node shows the earliest date at which the whole project can be concluded. The latest finish time (LFT) records the time by which the previous activity must be completed if the entire project is not to be delayed.

CPA offers businesses several advantages:
- It encourages managers to engage in detailed planning, which helps reduce the risk of delays and other problems.
- Resources needed for each activity may be made available at the appropriate time and so reduce costs, in particular the need for working capital.
- Time can be saved by operating certain activities simultaneously — possibly offering competitive advantage.
- The information from CPA assists managers in making high-quality decisions.

But, as with many techniques in business, there are disadvantages. These include:
- Complex activities may be impossible to represent accurately on a network.
- The project still requires management even after the initial network is drawn, as external factors may change.
- CPA relies on estimates for the expected duration of activities — if these are inaccurate, the whole process may be invalidated.

Analysis Opportunities for analysis exist in the following areas:
- constructing and interpreting a CPA network
- analysing the implications for businesses of the use of CPA
- arguing the benefits that a firm might gain from the use of CPA, particularly in relation to business decision-making
- highlighting the drawbacks that may arise from the use of CPA
- calculating variables such as EST, LFT and float (any spare time existing within an activity)

Evaluation A number of evaluative themes may be explored, including:
- assessing the impact of the use of CPA on the competitive performance of the business
- judging the significance of CPA in the development of a new product or major project
- evaluating the value of CPA in specific circumstances

> **Links** CPA relates closely to many areas of the specification, as it is an important technique of decision-making. You could therefore explore links with finance, marketing and other aspects of operations management.

Controlling operations and facilities

Information technology (IT) and organisations

Developments in IT create opportunities and pose threats for businesses. The effective use of IT can improve a business's performance in many ways. For example:

- IT can assist businesses in gaining knowledge of changes in the markets in which they trade. IT can monitor consumers' purchasing behaviour.
- In the form of Computer Aided Design (CAD) and Computer Aided Manufacture (CAM), IT can improve productivity and quality within manufacturing organisations.
- IT (and more specifically Management Information Systems) can allow effective communication within an organisation, thereby improving the quality of decision-making.
- Effective use of IT can facilitate delayering by allowing relatively junior employees access to information (e.g. budgetary data) necessary for decision-making.
- IT (and especially the internet) has opened up new markets and selling opportunities for businesses.
- IT can be a catalyst for changing working practices. A significant proportion of the UK's workforce is engaged in teleworking, in which technology allows employees to operate away from their employer's premises.

Threats exist too. These include:

- Developments in IT pose a threat to some established businesses. For example, some mail order companies have been hard hit by online selling.
- IT has fuelled the globalisation of markets. It is possible for overseas firms to sell into the UK using the internet without having a retail presence. This could become important in industries such as banking.
- Firms from other regions, or even countries, may poach employees and particularly those involved in teleworking. This development makes it more difficult for small firms to retain talented and skilled employees.

IT is more likely to be successful if:

- the use of IT is carefully planned to assist the organisation in achieving its objectives
- all employees receive appropriate and timely training
- managers select reliable equipment that is compatible with other systems already existing in the organisation

Location

The location of any business depends upon a variety of factors. Typical influences are:

- the proximity of natural resources, components and other supplies
- the infrastructure available in a particular locality
- the whereabouts of the market into which a business sells its products
- government actions, e.g. grants and other forms of financial support
- qualitative factors, such as the quality of life senior employees might expect from working and living in a particular location

Profit-making businesses will seek to identify the least-cost location. It is quite usual for firms to use financial techniques to assess the suitability of one or more locations. For example:

- Break-even analysis can be used to calculate costs and revenues of possible locations and the level of sales required for profitability.
- Investment appraisal techniques can be used to select the location offering the greatest return over a specified period of time.

International location

Firms taking decisions on international locations will consider a number of important factors:

- effective communications systems and transport networks
- trained and productive labour available at relatively low rates of pay
- low rates of taxation levied on business profits
- grants and concessions available from local and national governments to support the heavy investment necessary
- availability of support services (e.g. components, R&D)

They may also take into account a number of broader issues. For example:

- Is the country in which they are considering locating politically stable? Obviously, a firm does not want to risk any form of disruption to its activities.
- Is the company likely to suffer from exchange rate fluctuations as a consequence of its decision? This might be an argument for locating in countries using the euro.
- Will the company avoid tariffs or other trade barriers by locating in a particular country? One of the attractions for foreign businesses of locating in the UK is that they operate within the EU's Common External Tariff.

Analysis Opportunities for analysis exist in a number of areas:

- examining the advantages and disadvantages of introducing technology into a business
- analysing the factors a firm might consider when taking a decision on location
- considering the factors a multinational firm would take into account when considering a location decision
- calculating the least-cost location for a firm in specific circumstances

Evaluation There are several opportunities for evaluation in this area of the specification, including:

- weighing up the case for a business introducing information technology into some aspect or aspects of its operations
- assessing the 'best' location for a firm in a particular scenario
- evaluating the most important factor(s) in a particular business's location decisions

Links There are links with all other areas of the specification. It is possible to discover links with marketing, finance, people, objectives and strategy, as well as external influences.

Questions
&
Answers

In this section there are four case studies and associated questions. Each case study is accompanied by two sample answers interspersed with examiner's comments.

Questions

The questions are based on the format of the A2 papers. Unit 4 is different from Units 5 and 6 in a number of important ways:

- It covers two modules of the A2 specification — Modules 4 and 5.
- It is based on a case study of approximately 1000 words plus associated questions.
- There are four questions accompanying the case study (which might be sub-divided). Each question is worth 20 marks and there will be one question on each of the following areas of the specification: marketing, accounting and finance, people and organisations, and operations management.

Tackle the questions in this book to develop your examination technique, allowing yourself 90 minutes to answer all parts of each question. By considering the specimen answers provided and the examiner comments, you will be able to see how these questions may be answered effectively, and so avoid the potential pitfalls.

A common problem for students (and teachers) when completing a topic is the lack of examination questions that cover only the topic in question. These questions have been tailored so students can apply their knowledge and practise skills whilst topics are still relatively fresh in their minds, rather than wait until they have studied all of Modules 4 and 5 before being able to tackle a Unit 4 question paper.

Questions 1 to 3 are focused on specific areas of subject content as covered in the Content Guidance section of this guide. These questions may be tackled during the course, or on completion of the revision of that area of the specification. Question 4 is integrated, exactly mirroring the format of the Unit 4 examination with one question on each of the four areas of the specification: marketing, accounting and finance, people and organisations, and operations management. Remember, you will always be given credit for using business concepts from outside Unit 4, provided their use is entirely relevant to the question.

Sample answers

Resist the temptation to study the answers before you have attempted the questions. In each case, the first answer (by candidate A) is intended to show the type of response that would earn a grade A on that paper. This does not mean perfection — these answers are intended to show the range of responses that can earn high marks. In business studies, it is the quality of reasoning that is rewarded. Candidate B's answers demonstrate responses that are worthy of a pass, but at a lower grade.

Examiner's comments

The examiner's comments are preceded by the icon ℮. They are interspersed in the answers and indicate where credit is due. In the weaker answers, they also point out areas for improvement, specific problems and common errors.

Marketing

Friasco

Friasco plc is one of the success stories of the mobile telephone revolution. The company's origins lie in the development and manufacture of a range of electronic equipment for the computer and telecommunications industries. The company had enjoyed rising sales and profits, as technological products became essential items in the working lives and leisure activities of many UK consumers.

The change of direction

Chief executive Mary Fewster had a vision, however. In 1993 she proposed to the Friasco's board that the company should switch increasing amounts of resources into designing and manufacturing mobile telephones for a new generation of consumers.

The main points of Mary's plan were to:
- maintain current levels of sales for general electronic equipment, but seek to manufacture mobile telephones for use on networks such as that operated by Vodafone
- purchase a new factory on a nearby site in Coventry to manufacture the phones
- work jointly with a design company to develop a new and attractive range of products aimed at younger consumers
- seek agreements with major retailers to stock and promote these new products

From this development, Mary proposed a marketing strategy that would attract many new consumers from the younger age groups. The product was to be fun as well as functional, and new pricing methods were to be adopted to make the product more accessible. Friasco's products would be available in a wide range of retail outlets.

She argued persuasively that the mobile telephone market was ripe for change. 'I do not have the results of market research to place in front of you. My proposal is not based upon any real market analysis — it is based on instinct, gathered over 25 years in the technology industry. The mobile phone industry is ripe for change. There are huge numbers of potential consumers out there who might purchase mobile phones if they are promoted in the right way and at affordable prices. I am aware of the degree of risk in this proposal, but this is matched by the potential returns we might expect.'

She continued: 'The sales forecasts produced by the marketing department (*shown in Appendix A*) indicate the possibilities that exist in this market. I think that this is the start of something big and we can transform this company if we take a bold decision now. Leaving this until later will be too late — other firms will be established in the market and consumer loyalty will be difficult to overturn.'

question

Keeping ahead of the game

The Fewster plan was a success beyond all expectations. Friasco produced a range of mobile phones that had enormous appeal to the growing numbers of consumers. By 2000 the annual sales of mobile phones in the UK were over 20 million — well ahead of the original forecasts. Friasco had enjoyed a steadily rising share of the market, gaining a reputation for manufacturing high-quality telephones that were fun and functional. In 2000 the company sold over 8 million phones in the UK alone and mounted a real challenge to the pre-eminence of Nokia in this particular market.

The Board of Friasco was alert to developments in the market for mobile phones. By 2001 it was apparent that the years of increasing growth in demand for mobile phones were drawing to a close: the market was saturated. Friasco's competitors were taking steps to sell surplus phones and to remove excess capacity. The new generation of mobile phones was receiving much attention in the media and offered a tantalising prospect for Friasco, even though the growth of sales of these new phones was expected to be slower than in the past.

Mary Fewster was determined that the company should adjust its marketing strategy to reflect the changing market circumstances. 'The new generation of mobile phones are on the way,' she said. 'This is now a more mature and complex market and we should research it carefully in order to benefit from accurate sales forecasts. This would be money well spent. I am convinced that an effective marketing function is the vital element of the continued success of Friasco in a changing marketplace.'

The Board approved a major increase in the company's marketing budget to allow a thorough analysis of the changing market for mobile telephones. This increased budget was also intended to allow the company to adjust its marketing mix. The company's marketing strategy was revised to cope with the particular demands of a saturated market and overcapacity.

Year	UK market size (millions)	Friasco sales forecasts (millions)
1990	0.54	–
1991	0.88	–
1992	1.03	–
1993	1.89	–
1994	2.01	0.20
1995	2.92	0.65
1996	4.15	1.25
1997	5.85	2.24
1998	7.71	3.15
1999	11.75	4.38
2000	14.02	6.86

Appendix A:
UK sales of mobile phones 1990–2000, and anticipated sales for Friasco. (Compiled by Friasco in 1993 with forecast figures in italics.)

(1) (a) Examine how Friasco's marketing department might have produced its
original sales forecast. *(8 marks)*
(b) Assess the case for and against Friasco investing heavily in producing
accurate sales forecasts. *(12 marks)*
(2) Mary's instincts determined Friasco's new marketing strategy. Discuss whether
it is appropriate for a large manufacturing company to base its marketing
strategy on the instincts of a single senior employee. *(20 marks)*
(3) (a) Analyse the ways in which Friasco might adjust its marketing mix to cope
with the demands of a saturated market. *(8 marks)*
(b) Discuss the possible influences on Friasco's marketing budget for the
forthcoming financial year. *(12 marks)*
(4) Mary Fewster argues that 'an effective marketing function is the vital element
of the continued success of Friasco in a changing marketplace'. To what
extent do you agree with her view? *(20 marks)*

Total: 80 marks

■ ■ ■

Answer to question 1: candidate A

(1) (a) Friasco could have used the techniques of extrapolation to forecast the future
sales of mobile phones in the UK. This entails identifying the trend in the data and
simply extending it forward into the future, possibly just by eye. This would be a
simple strategy for the company, being both quick and cheap. However, it has a
number of drawbacks, especially in a new and rapidly changing market such as
that for mobile telephones. In such a volatile market, the past is not a good
indicator of the future. In fact, the company's original forecast underestimated the
rate of increase in demand for mobile phones.

A better approach might have been to conduct market research to establish
consumers' intentions and use this information as the basis of sales forecasts.
This uses current information to predict the future and may have given some
indication of the growth that was to occur in the market for mobile phones. It
would, however, have taken time and to produce accurate forecasts may have
been expensive. The delay necessary to gain accurate information may have been
inappropriate in the circumstances facing Friasco in 1993.

🖉 This is a good answer. It is well structured in that the candidate has developed a
couple of arguments fully. The candidate has used relevant knowledge (of the advantages and disadvantages of techniques of making sales forecasts) in developing his
response and has also applied this knowledge effectively to the scenario. For
example, the candidate has stressed the weakness of extrapolation of data in a
volatile market, drawing on data from the text to substantiate the argument.

(b) Friasco would benefit from investing in generating accurate sales forecasts in
that it would be able to schedule production to meet the level of sales. This would
avoid the costs of storing unsold mobile phones (which could become obsolete),

49

though at least the products are not large and bulky. Equally, it would avoid the embarrassment of being unable to fulfil orders and thereby losing out to competitors such as Nokia.

But to create accurate sales forecasts might be expensive, or even an impossibility in a changeable market such as that for mobile phones in the years after 2001. The company may find it necessary to spend heavily on market research, which may even then not prove accurate. This could be particularly true if large competitors such as Nokia or Ericsson behave in unpredictable ways.

> This response is not of the highest standard, but nevertheless contains a number of pleasing features. Candidate A has recognised the two sides of the argument and addressed these effectively by developing arguments in two paragraphs. The candidate has also related the answers to the scenario in the case study throughout. However, an evaluative conclusion has not been provided.

(2) A marketing strategy is a plan of the future marketing activities in which a firm will engage. It is intended to assist the company in achieving its objectives. A marketing strategy involves managers in identifying the business's objectives, analysing the business and the market in which it operates as well as assessing the resources that the business has available to it.

Friasco relied upon Mary Fewster's instinct in planning its original strategy and this was not a risk in that she had a clear understanding of the business — she set the business's objectives and must have had a clear understanding of the business's financial and other strengths and weaknesses. Knowing the business so well and having an appreciation of its sense of direction, using Mary Fewster's instinct to establish strategy does make sense to some degree.

However, the weakness in this argument is that Friasco had not analysed the market properly. Mary had a hunch that demand for mobile phones from young people would grow rapidly and that the product they wanted would differ. This was at the core of Friasco's strategy. This represented a considerable risk given that a large investment was necessary to carry out the switch to increased mobile phone production. It would have made sense for such a major decision to be based upon careful analysis of the market, ensuring that the research focused upon the groups in the population who were expected to become the new consumers. This might have introduced a more quantifiable element into the strategy and reduced the amount of guesswork and risk.

Whether this is appropriate depends upon the degree of risk that the strategy involves. For Friasco this might have been acceptable in that the company was profitable before the decision and was intending to retain its profitable elements. The new strategy was really an addition, and was based on the judgement of an experienced and successful manager. It might have been appropriate to use investment appraisal techniques (once market research was complete) to assess the worth of the investment.

🖉 This is a well-constructed answer that is relevant throughout. Candidate A puts forward arguments for and against the notion of basing strategy on a manager's instincts — in particular highlighting the lack of market analysis. This is a sensible and effective format. Having noted the arguments on either side, the candidate offers some overall judgement set in the context of the case study. The comment about investment analysis is valid — although this is a marketing question, it is perfectly acceptable to bring in other relevant subject matter.

(3) (a) A saturated market means that most consumers who want a particular product have already purchased it. There will be few new purchasers, with most buyers seeking replacement products. Firms will have to think of new ways in which to present their products to persuade consumers to purchase them.

The marketing mix is also called the 'four Ps': price, product, place and promotion. These can be altered to persuade consumers to buy more of a product or to respond to the actions of competitors. The marketing mix is a series of tactics which allow a business to fulfil its marketing objectives.

It is probable that Friasco will have to cut its prices to sell its products in large quantities. It may also need to carry out more promotion. Finally, Friasco may need to think about its methods of distribution to help overcome the saturation of the market.

🖉 This was surprising given the quality of this candidate's earlier answers. This answer is strong in terms of subject knowledge in that the candidate explains the meanings of the key terms very effectively. This represented a fair start, but the candidate then really failed to address the question. The answer could have considered more carefully the possible effects of cutting prices. For example, how might competitors respond and what might be the value of price elasticity of demand? Similarly, the candidate should also have explained how promotion might help in these circumstances, plus any possible drawbacks.

(b) The company's marketing budget will be affected by the circumstances in which it finds itself. Introducing a major new product range will require expenditure on market research to identify the exact needs of consumers as far as is possible. Once developed, the new mobile phones will need substantial promotion and PR work with the service providers such as Orange and Vodafone. These factors will tend to push up the amount the company allocates to its marketing budget.

The company's financial position will, of course, directly affect the amount it spends on marketing. Friasco has high levels of sales and profits, so this will enable the firm to fund advertising campaigns and public relations activities to a greater extent than might otherwise have been possible.

The reactions of competitors and the amount they spend will be the most important factors. Friasco is looking to break into a new market and will have to at least match (and probably exceed) the marketing expenditure of rivals such as Nokia if it is to become established. If Nokia or Ericsson decide to invest in a major marketing campaign, Friasco will be obliged to respond to ensure that consumers' awareness of its products increases.

🖉 Here is another good answer. It identifies a number of relevant factors and uses them in the context of the case study. Candidate A responds to the command word in the question ('discuss', which calls for evaluation) by making a justified judgement in the final paragraph.

(4) The marketing function is a wide range of activities including setting marketing objectives, market research, marketing planning and marketing activities, such as promotion and pricing. This is very important to Friasco, as it will assist the company in discovering consumers' needs and making sure that its products meet these needs. Thus the company should undertake market research to make certain its products are right for the market. Without this, in what is a rapidly changing marketplace, Friasco's phone could become obsolete or (given its target market) unfashionable.

But other functions within the business are equally important. Friasco operates in a high-technology business and one in which the technology changes very rapidly. It is vital that the company's products are at the cutting edge of the new technology to maintain their appeal to the younger groups in society. This means that continual research and development is essential to maintain the company's prime position in this market. The case study emphasises that change is occurring with a new generation of mobile phones, highlighting the necessity of an effective R&D function.

It is also possible to argue that production is a vital element in the future success of the company. Friasco wants to acquire a reputation for producing high-quality phones with minimal numbers of defects. Such quality is essential to satisfy the demands of the large retail outlets purchasing and selling the phones — they do not want customers returning faulty phones and making complaints. Production plays an important role in minimising costs, enabling the business to price competitively in the market.

Marketing is very important to the future success of Friasco. The company is...

🖉 This is a response of mixed quality. The answer contains some good analysis explaining why marketing — or other functions within the business — might be central to its continued success. However, the candidate obviously ran out of time and did not offer an evaluation of the answer. This shortage of time came about because some earlier responses were lengthy and because the scope of this answer was too ambitious. Realising the shortage of time, the candidate should have included an evaluation in the third paragraph.

🖉 **This is a strong grade-A answer. At times the quality is a little variable, but candidate A has good subject knowledge and a clear understanding of the skills necessary to gain a high grade.**

■ ■ ■

Answer to question 1: candidate B

(1) (a) Friasco could have produced its sales forecasts in a number of ways. The company might have asked large numbers of people who might buy the products what they thought of its ideas and how many of the phones they would purchase. This could be done through a random sample where everyone in the population has an equal chance of being asked. On the other hand, it could be a selected sample where people are chosen carefully because they are likely to be consumers. Another method is using previous sales figures as a guide to next year's sales.

> ✍ This is not a well-organised answer. Candidate B has written a single paragraph containing a number of ideas that are relevant but not used effectively. The candidate has recognised that previous sales data and market research are important methods of forecasting sales, but has not really applied this knowledge to the circumstances of the question. Some analysis of the benefits and drawbacks of the two approaches would have improved the quality of these answers. Why, for example, are previous sales figures of little use to Friasco? It is worth comparing this response to that of Candidate A.

(b) The company could spend money on conducting a lot of market research to discover the numbers of people who might buy the mobile phones. This would help the company in planning its production. It would help the business to purchase the right amount of materials and to hire the correct numbers of employees. The firm would be able to rent or buy another factory if necessary and would always be able to meet the demand for the phones.

The company could use this information to help it to decide whether it is worth going ahead to produce particular brands of mobile phones. If the forecasts indicate low sales it might be that there are insufficient sales to reach break-even level of output and Friasco might decide to abandon the product rather than to lose money producing and advertising the new mobile phone.

> ✍ This is another mediocre answer. First, candidate B only really addresses one side of the question, concentrating solely on the benefits to Friasco of producing accurate sales forecasts. The candidate fails to develop the arguments, for example by analysing clearly the ways in which the company might benefit from being able to plan production effectively. The second paragraph presents a better-quality argument, but the line of thought is not followed through. Candidate B also fails to write evaluatively — always more difficult when only one side of an argument is considered.

(2) Friasco developed a marketing strategy to try and reach its marketing objectives. The company's objectives are to develop a share of the growing market for mobile telephones and the strategy is designed to achieve this.

I think that it is appropriate for the business to do this because it is based on the judgement of an experienced employee who has been in the industry for 25 years and understands it well. Also she knows all about the company. This approach gave the company an advantage as it was a bit late entering the mobile phone market and needed to make a quick decision. This approach saved using time on market research and talking to consumers — time which was needed to create new phones.

The marketing strategy was carefully planned to fit with the company's overall corporate objectives of growth through entering a new and expanding market. It also built upon the existing strengths of the company, so it was consistent.

> Candidate B had a fair knowledge of relevant subject matter, but didn't really make the best use of it, failing to develop arguments fully. The first paragraph provides a clear example of this. The candidate did not develop the drawbacks of operating on instinct until the latter stages of the answer — only belatedly appreciating the full scope of the question.

(3) (a) The marketing mix is price, place, promotion and product. Friasco might alter its mix in the following ways.

It is likely to have to reduce the price of its products to persuade consumers who haven't bought a mobile phone at an earlier time to do so. Consumers may also decide to replace phones bought earlier with a newer model. By reducing its prices Friasco would possibly win a greater market share dependent upon the reactions of rivals. So long as demand for mobile phones is price elastic and competitors do not undercut them, this approach might be successful.

The company will almost certainly have to increase the level of promotions. Special offers and persuasive campaigns will help to win more customers so long as they are well designed and targeted accurately at potential consumers. However, Friasco's competitors will probably be doing the same thing, so a distinctive advertising campaign would be particularly useful in these circumstances.

> This is a good-quality answer and better than any other response so-far by candidate B. The candidate identifies the elements of the marketing mix and then relates the changes necessary to the situation of the market in which Friasco is trading. One of the strengths of this answer is that candidate B considers the possible problems that might be encountered by adjusting the marketing mix in the ways proposed.

(b) Friasco will use its marketing budget to pay for advertising, promotions and public relations. It may also be used for market research. The main factor that will influence the company in setting its marketing budget is the marketing objectives of the business. Friasco has the objective of analysing the situation within a changing market and then planning a suitable approach to continue the company's success. This is likely to involve heavy expenditure on market research and test marketing to discover the nature of consumers' needs. Test marketing will confirm whether or not proposed products will meet with the requirements of the market.

The amount of money spent on marketing activities over the past year is also likely to influence the decision on the budget. If rival firms invest in heavy advertising or well-publicised special offers, then Friasco will have to respond or risk losing its share of what is a declining market. It is likely that firms will have been increasing their marketing expenditure once they have recognised the saturation of the market and this will be a significant pressure on Friasco and the other companies in the mobile phone manufacturing market. This will probably be the most important factor.

e This is a good attempt at answering the question. Candidate B has written two analytical paragraphs examining the factors that might influence Friasco managers when taking a decision on the marketing budget. These are well argued, but the candidate has not made any worthwhile attempt to evaluate the relative importance of these factors, simply saying that one will 'be the most important factor' without justifying this view.

(4) Friasco's marketing function will be an important factor determining its success. The business will need to discover what it is that consumers want in the near future. The firm will need to research the market for mobile telephones to identify the future pattern of demand and to make sure that its products are suitable for consumers over the next few years. This will ensure that they get the product right.

The company will also have to make sure that it prices its products competitively to ensure that consumers do not decide to purchase the products of a competitor. This may be a particular problem if Friasco's phones are similar to those produced by other companies, for example Motorola. In this case demand will be price elastic.

Finally, the amount and quality of promotion will be very important in determining the future success of the business. Consumers need to know about the new products Friasco is producing if they are to purchase them. It is also important to publicise the quality and features of the new phones to ensure that they are bought in sufficient quantity.

e This is a disappointing answer and of lower quality than the response to question 3. Candidate B has only responded to one side of the question. The candidate has also interpreted marketing very narrowly, focusing mainly on the marketing mix and not discussing important activities such as setting marketing objectives and developing a strategy. Candidate B has not considered the other functions of the business that may be important in the circumstances of a saturated and changing market. Once again the one-sided nature of the argument has made it very difficult for the candidate to evaluate effectively.

e **Candidate B has a reasonable knowledge of marketing but has not consistently shown the skills essential to achieve a high grade on this unit. The answers to the two parts of question 3 are of good quality, but other answers are somewhat weaker. This script would be worthy of a grade C.**

Accounting and finance

Velocity plc

Velocity was going through a tough time. As one of the UK's leading train and coach operators, it enjoyed considerable success following the privatisation of rail services in the early 1990s. Velocity won the franchise to operate trains in the west of England and Wales. Unlike other rail operators, it also had a reputation for arriving on time and for providing a comfortable and speedy service.

Velocity's managing director David Summers had excellent public relations skills and was very successful in dealing with the media. David had worked in transport companies in Hong Kong and Canada before coming back to the UK to head up the company bidding for the franchises to operate trains on a number of routes. Velocity had run coach services for many years, but was looking to expand its business. Running train services seemed a natural development for a transport business.

Velocity had been a strong performer on the Stock Exchange, offering investors excellent returns and promising substantial growth in the years ahead. Recently the company's fortunes have foundered for a number of reasons. The company's decision to purchase hotels throughout Ireland seemed risky and events appear to have proved the critics correct. Concerns were expressed about the way in which the company financed its growth by the use of borrowed money, making Velocity vulnerable to interest rate rises. Shareholders began to wonder whether they had been influenced by the charm of the managing director rather than the potential of the business.

By 2001 David Summers and Velocity were under pressure. The company's sales had stagnated, profits were down and the quality of service seemed to have declined. Passenger groups were complaining about late trains and dirty carriages. Velocity appeared to have lost its sense of purpose. At a board meeting towards the end of the year, David put forward a number of plans to his fellow directors.

He explained that a holiday company, Eurotours, had asked Velocity to provide transport for its European coach holidays. David noted that this would make more effective use of Velocity's fleet of coaches (which had been underused in recent years), but commented that the daily rate on offer was not attractive. 'We normally receive £500 a day for a coach and driver. Eurotours is only offering £400. I estimate the fixed costs associated with this project to be £160,000. The good news is that this could amount to 1800 days' work each year.' He concluded that the costs (set out in Appendix C) were difficult to estimate. 'Fuel costs might vary and the transport market is very changeable: it is equally difficult to predict prices and costs.'

This was not the item of most interest to David Summers, however. 'There are two issues I want to draw to your attention. We need to improve our appeal to the investors in the City. One way to do this is to expand our operations in exciting and profitable ways. I have two proposals. Southern Trains is about to lose its franchise to operate train services in the south and southwest of England. I believe we should bid for the franchise. It would complement our operations elsewhere, and I am advised that the government would look favourably on any application we might make.'

'It is the other proposal which really excites me,' David admitted. 'I still have a lot of contacts from my time in Canada and I have been asked whether we would be interested in participating in a joint venture to provide a light rail service for the cities of Montreal and Ottawa and surrounding districts. A local company, Brunswick Rail, is keen to have our financial support and to benefit from our expertise. I don't think we are able to take on the franchise and to put resources into the Canadian enterprise. We have to choose between these alternatives,' he concluded.

Other members of the Board did not share his enthusiasm. Several were unconvinced by the attractions of either project and questioned the wisdom of the company considering large-scale investments at this time.

Appendix A Forecast cash flows for the two alternative investments

Year	Brunswick Rail (Canadian investment) Net cash flows (£m)	Southern Trains (rail franchise) Net cash flows (£m)
2002	(300)	(200)
2003	89	60
2004	121	65
2005	131	65
2006	144	110

Appendix B Accounts for Velocity plc (Year to March 2002)

Profit and loss account (year to March 2002)		Balance sheet as at 31 March 2002	
	£m		£m
Turnover	**606.4**	**Fixed assets**	**811.3**
Cost of sales	371.4	Stock	33.5
Gross profit	**235.0**	Debtors	13.1
Overheads	115.7	Cash	19.4
Depreciation	12.9	Creditors	71.1
Operating profit	**106.4**	**Net current assets**	**(5.1)**
One-off item	4.3	**Net assets employed**	**806.2**
Pre-tax profit	**102.1**	Long-term loans	296.6
		Share capital	329.5
		Reserves	180.1
		Capital employed	**806.2**

Appendix C Costs of supplying coach services

Cost	Daily rate (£)
Drivers' wages (including overtime)	115
Average fuel costs	100
Other costs	85

(1) (a) Using the data available to you, calculate whether or not Velocity should take up the offer from Eurotours. (6 marks)

(b) Assess the value of break-even analysis to Velocity in reaching a decision on whether to accept Eurotour's offer. (14 marks)

(2) (a) Calculate the following ratios for Velocity:
- gearing ratio
- return on capital employed (5 marks)

(b) Using your answers to the first part of the question and the other evidence in the case, suggest how Velocity should raise a large sum of capital to invest in either of the projects. You should justify your answer. (15 marks)

(3) (a) Using the average rate of return method of investment appraisal, compare the returns from the Canadian investment and the rail franchise. On the basis of your calculations, propose which investment is the more attractive. (10 marks)

(b) Discuss the potential value of investment appraisal techniques to Velocity in these circumstances. (10 marks)

(4) (a) Examine how the final accounts of Velocity might be made more attractive to potential investors. (8 marks)

(b) Discuss whether the existence of risk means that it is unwise for managers to make decisions on the basis of financial data. (12 marks)

Total: 80 marks

■ ■ ■

Answer to question 2: candidate A

(1) (a) The break-even point for the Eurotours offer is 1,600 days work. So, if Eurotours hire Velocity's coaches for more than this number of days, the project will earn a profit. As David expects that the firm will require coaches for 1,800 days, it looks as though Velocity should accept the offer.

    ☑ This is an entirely correct answer. The calculation is correct and the decision, based upon the figures, is right. However, this is a high-risk strategy. Had there been an error, a lot of marks would have been lost because it would have been impossible to follow the candidate's reasoning and to award marks for process. It is always advisable to show calculations when answering this type of question.

(b) Break-even gives a number of advantages to a business. The figure provides a rule of thumb and is very useful for new businesses or new enterprises. It can help a firm to reach a decision on whether a particular project is worthwhile and likely to prove profitable. It is quick and simple to conduct and without it many businesses would operate on the basis of hunches or guesses.

But it also has many weaknesses. The theory assumes that a firm will sell all of its output, and this is a major assumption. Some production may remain unsold. Although it can cope with changing circumstances, it is restricted to firm's charging a single price and it cannot cope with regular variations in costs.

This is a technique that has some uses, so long as its limitations are borne in mind. It is better than nothing.

🖉 Candidate A has committed a common error in answering this question. The candidate has entirely ignored the scenario and has produced a textbook answer. Marks for applying a response to the context of the question would not be awarded. This also partly explains why the candidate found difficulty in evaluating — there was information in the case study that may have been helpful in this respect.

(2) (a) Velocity's ratios are as follows:

$$\text{gearing} = \frac{\text{long-term loans}}{\text{capital employed}} \times 100\% = \frac{296.6 \times 100\%}{806.2} = 36.79\%$$

$$\text{ROCE} = \frac{\text{operating profit}}{\text{capital employed}} \times 100\% = \frac{106.4 \times 100\%}{806.2} = 13.20\%$$

🖉 This is excellent. Candidate A has shown knowledge of the formulae and has carried both calculations through correctly. This time the answer includes the candidates' workings in case of arithmetical error.

(b) Velocity needs to raise at least £200 million and possibly £300 million. Almost certainly it will require more than a single source of finance for this. The company's gearing ratio is relatively encouraging in that it is significantly below 50%. If the company opted to borrow the full £200 million to purchase the Southern Trains franchise, this would only take the gearing ratio to 496.6 × 100/1006.2 = 49.35%, which is just about an acceptable figure. This would, however, make Velocity more vulnerable to interest rate rises.

A proportion of the money should be raised through a share issue, which would assist the company's gearing ratio, but this may prove tricky in the light of the latest return on capital figure of 13.2%. This will not impress investors and the managers might have to sell the shares at a discount to attract sufficient buyers — a rights issue might be the answer.

Thus, given the amount of capital required and the low figure for ROCE, I would suggest a combination of long-term loans and share capital.

question

📝 This is a good response and an interesting comparison to candidate A's answer to 1(b). This response draws heavily upon the material in the text and mixes it well with relevant theory. The candidate also makes effective use of the answers to the previous question. This was important information and was handled particularly well.

(3) (a) The annual average rates of return for the two projects are as follows.

	Rail franchise	Canadian project
Cost of project (£m)	200	300
Revenue (£m)	300	485
Profits (£m)	100	185
Annual profit (£m)	25	46.25
Annual rate of return (%)	12.5	15.41

On the basis on these calculations, I would recommend that Velocity should invest in the Canadian project as the return is expected to be nearly 2% higher.

📝 Here is another good answer. The presentation is much better than the answer to question 1(a). The workings have been clearly shown and the results interpreted by saying which investment was preferable according to these calculations.

(b) Investment appraisal techniques include payback, the average rate of return and net present value. These are all useful in assessing and comparing investment projects on the basis of financial data. Thus Velocity can compare the two projects as in the previous answer and make a relatively accurate decision on the basis of numerical data. Using the annual rate of return provides a figure allowing comparison with the general rate of interest and providing further guidance in decision-making. If Velocity chose to use a discounted cash flow technique, this would take into account the timing of the expenditures and receipts, giving a more accurate comparison. These techniques provide a quantitative measure to help firms take decisions on investment programmes, often against a background of uncertainty.

However, there are many factors not covered by investment appraisal techniques. All of these approaches are useless unless the data used in them are accurate. We have no indication of the source of Velocity's data, but any revenue forecasts in the transport industry are not likely to be entirely accurate. A bad rail crash or rising prosperity, leading to more car owners, could reduce its revenue considerably. There might, for example, be environmental issues associated with building a light rail network in Canada that would not show up in the calculations carried out as part of investment appraisal. Building a track across some unspoilt countryside may mean that nearby residents face costs which are not in the ARR calculation.

Investment appraisal techniques might be particularly valuable to Velocity. The company is comparing two very different projects, so bringing some structure to the comparison is helpful. However, issues such as exchange rates (for the Canadian project) may complicate the matter.

> ✎ This answer is well argued. Candidate A recognises that investment decisions should be taken on the basis of quantitative and qualitative information. The argument acknowledges the importance of both factors and consistently relates the theory to the circumstances faced by Velocity. The final paragraph contains some attempt at evaluation, which would have benefited from some further development.

(4) (a) Window dressing involves improving the look of a business's accounts in ways that are not illegal. Velocity could use window dressing in two main ways. The company's cash position is rather insecure with an acid test ratio of 0.46. Velocity's managers could sell a fixed asset (and perhaps lease it back) just prior to the drawing up of the balance sheet. This would give an injection of cash to the firm, making it more liquid and attractive to investors.

Velocity's operating profits are not very impressive. The company has a relatively low return on capital and could benefit from an improved profit figure. Velocity's managers could achieve this by bringing forward payment for goods in the final weeks of the financial year. By boosting revenue in this way the company's profit figure may be 'massaged' — investors would be more impressed by the prospect of high dividends and rising share values. However, the revenue figure for the following trading year would be reduced by a corresponding amount.

> ✎ This is a very impressive answer. Candidate A has used knowledge of window dressing and wider financial issues and has applied them effectively to the context of the case study. The calculation of the acid test ratio to highlight Velocity's need to enhance its liquidity position, prior to suggesting how this might be achieved, is high-quality writing.

(b) Risk is any threat to the continuation of a business's trading activities. Risk is identifiable and in some circumstances may be measurable. This is different from uncertainty, which is unpredictable and not quantifiable.

Risk does not invalidate the results of financial forecasts because an allowance for risk is built into many forecasts. Thus a manager might opt to reduce slightly the sales forecasts for the forthcoming financial year to represent the risk of a fall in demand. This action will depress forecast revenues and profits.

Risk attached to the trading activities of firms can be measured using financial data. Ratios such as the acid test and gearing measure the risk of firms having too little cash or borrowing too much and becoming vulnerable to rising interest rates.

But the existence of risk cannot always be measured and therefore will not necessarily be included in all financial data. Changing costs or lower prices from competitors might be entirely unexpected, as might a crisis. For example, Coca-

Cola's supplies of its famous soft drink in Belgium became contaminated and this led to a slump in sales across Europe. This type of risk is difficult to identify and incorporate into financial data.

However, a well-managed firm will have contingency plans in place to deal with unexpected happenings — this should permit a firm to deal with the element of risk that is difficult to measure. Measurable risks will be built into financial data and especially financial forecasts. Decisions should be taken with confidence...

🖉 This was a challenging question. Candidate A dealt with it confidently, starting by explaining the nature of risk. The candidate tackled both sides of the question, offering arguments supporting the statement in the question and also proposing the alternative viewpoint. This was interesting and relevant and was absolutely dependent upon a thorough understanding of the nature of risk. At the end candidate A attempted to supply an evaluative conclusion, though obviously ran out of time.

🖉 **Overall, these answers would have earned candidate A a well-deserved grade A.**

■ ■ ■

Answer to question 2: candidate B

(1) (a) Velocity can easily calculate whether or not to accept the offer from Eurotours. The profits from the deal will be as follows:

Income = 1,800 × £400 = £720,000

Costs = 1,800 × £300 = £540,000

Profit = £720,000 − £540,000 = £180,000

Thus the deal will earn Velocity a great amount of profit and should be accepted.

🖉 This answer has some good features in that candidate B has used some of the data from the case study and has arrived at a reasonable answer. However, the candidate has omitted to include the fixed costs associated with the coach tours to Europe. This shows an incomplete understanding of how to calculate break-even or profits and is disappointing in a second-year A-level business studies student.

(b) Break-even has a lot of advantages for firms such as Velocity:
- It is a simple technique that most managers can use without any training.
- It is particularly suitable for small businesses.
- Break-even analysis can be useful in helping managers to negotiate a loan.
- Break-even analysis can be completed quickly, giving managers immediate results.
- Businesses can use break-even analysis to forecast profits or losses at various levels of output.

Break-even analysis can be applied in many circumstances and can cope with changes in costs and revenues.

2 This is a very poor answer. Candidate B has not thought about what the question requires. The candidate has simply listed information remembered from notes and has not attempted to use the information in any way. This answer has a number of other faults. No attempt has been made to develop the arguments used or to apply them to the scenario. To do so would have required raising fewer points. This was also necessary to allow the other side of the argument (the weaknesses of break-even) to be put and to offer an evaluative conclusion.

(2) (a) The ratios for Velocity are:

$$296.6/806.2 = 0.368 \text{ --- gearing}$$

$$106.4/806.2 = 0.132 \text{ --- return on capital}$$

2 Although this is essentially correct, the presentation is a bit careless. The candidate has not written down the formulae. It is a good idea to do this to earn basic marks for content as well as to help the process of calculation. Furthermore, each of these ratios should be expressed as a percentage --- candidate B did not multiply the results by 100 to arrive at the correct figure.

(b) The business could raise a large sum of capital in a number of ways. It could issue more shares as it is a public limited company. This will be a relatively cheap way of raising further funds, especially if it opts for a rights issue. This targets existing shareholders as purchasers of new shares and saves a lot of selling costs. The benefit of doing this is that Velocity is not committed to paying regular interest payments as it would be if it took out a loan from a bank. However, issuing more shares might mean that existing directors lose control of the business as new shareholders use their influence in voting at AGMs.

The firm could also raise more money through a long-term loan, possibly by mortgaging some of its property. This would be fairly easy to organise so long as the firm had sufficient assets and would not result in new shareholders. However, this could be an expensive option, especially if interest rates rise.

The first option would be preferable because the risk is lower in the event of interest rates fluctuating. I would recommend Velocity took this action.

2 This is a response of mixed quality. Candidate B follows the required format of the question to some extent, identifying and analysing the advantages and drawbacks of two methods of raising finance. The candidate also offers a judgement as to which option the company should choose. The weakness of the response is that it fails to consider the circumstances of the question and to make use (as requested) of the calculations completed in the first section of the answer.

(3) (a) The average rate of return for the two projects is as follows. The investment in the Canadian rail project will earn the company a profit of £185 million over 4 years or £46.25 million on average each year. This is a return of 15.41% in terms of the original investment.

In contrast, purchasing the franchise for Southern Trains will generate an annual profit of £25 million, giving a 12.5% return on the original investment. This would not be as attractive as the Ottawa–Montreal light railway as the returns are lower.

> A somewhat unconventional answer is given here in terms of presentation, but it is nevertheless correct. Candidate B should have shown all of the workings in case of an error in calculation. However, the candidate did precisely what the question asked for and interpreted the results correctly.

(b) Using techniques such as average rate of return or net present value assists Velocity's managers in reaching a decision on which investment to accept. The ARR allows the firm to compare the return with that earned by the other investment and also to compare it with the rate of interest. Neither of the returns is very high and it might be that Velocity does not consider them worthwhile. The returns may be reduced further if the money is borrowed and interest rates rise. Without techniques of investment appraisal, Velocity's managers would need to rely upon a hunch as to which was the best investment. In spite of David's experience in Canada, Velocity might find it difficult to judge the returns from investing in the Ottawa–Montreal light railway without researching data and comparing forecast costs and revenues.

Approaches such as the average rate of return balance the returns from an investment against the rewards and give an indication of the surplus (if any) that may exist. Earning maximum levels of profits is probably one of Velocity's objectives and using techniques which produce a profit figure is appropriate.

> This question has not been interpreted fully. Candidate B has put together some good arguments supporting the use of investment appraisal in this type of decision. The answer is set in the context of the question, making effective use of the scenario. Yet it is incomplete. Questions with 'discuss' as a command word require students to evaluate and, in this case, candidate B should have examined at least one argument against the use of investment appraisal techniques before making a judgement in a final paragraph.

(4) (a) Velocity could improve its accounts by increasing the profit margin on its products. This might reduce sales but would make more profit on every sale and would therefore improve the company's return on capital. If the company could reduce costs, it might also seem more profitable and attractive to investors.

The company could use window dressing. This is not illegal, but some firms consider this approach to be unethical. Velocity might decide to sell off a major asset such as an office block and then to rent it back from the buyer. This action would increase the amount of cash in the business, making the company look less risky to potential investors, and may improve the share price. However, many shareholders would understand techniques such as this and may not be impressed by the company taking this sort of step to disguise a financial weakness.

This is a typical answer to an examination question in one sense at least. The candidate did not think carefully about the question before starting to write. The first paragraph is not good. The candidate's suggestions on how to improve the look of the company's accounts could not be applied at the end of the financial year. They may also not work because demand may be very price elastic and profits may decline due to falling sales and the increased impact of fixed costs. The second paragraph is much better, as the candidate addresses the question directly and offers some evidence of theoretical understanding of the concept of window dressing. The answer does not, however, relate to the circumstances of Velocity in a clear manner. The specific ways needed to improve Velocity's accounts were requested.

(b) The use of financial techniques can help Velocity to assess the importance of risk when taking financial decisions. Without these techniques the business would not be able to build in any allowance for this factor. Companies may produce sales forecasts that make an allowance for risk, perhaps producing a lower figure than might otherwise be the case. The actual construction of financial forecasts may make managers think about the degree of risk that may be present. Without financial planning, risk might not be considered.

But financial data do not always accurately reflect risk. This is very difficult to measure and may occur in unexpected ways. It is also very difficult to quantify risk. How would a firm build the possibility of a new product unexpectedly appearing on the market into its financial forecasts?

Candidate B is not entirely clear about the nature of risk and how it might differ from uncertainty. The candidate makes a couple of reasonable points and recognises that this argument has two sides. What the answer fails to consider fully is that financial forecasts have much value for other reasons and that firms can adopt different techniques to cope with risk. This answer, as with candidate B's other answers, required a better structure — examining both sides of the argument before offering evaluation.

This set of answers is of variable quality. Candidate B has a fair knowledge of relevant subject matter, but is often unclear about what the questions require. This would be worth a grade D overall.

Question 3

People in organisations and operations management

Cosmetic changes

Wasim Akbar was adamant: 'We cannot stay as we are. The world is changing and we must change with it if we are to survive. The competition is getting tougher and we need to respond. If you don't agree with my plans, then offer better suggestions — if you can. To do nothing is not an option.'

The chief executive's challenge brought about a moment of quiet in what had been a stormy board meeting for Natura Products. The company, which floated on the Stock Exchange several years ago, remains the premier supplier of natural cosmetic products to UK retailers. Taking a strong environmental and ethical stance at its establishment in 1990, Natura was in tune with consumers' demands for products that were not tested on animals and did not exploit people or the environment in the Third World. Spectacular growth and lucrative contracts with high-street retailers such as Boots, Debenhams and John Lewis had followed. But by 1999 growth had come to a halt as increasing competition appeared, forcing prices for all cosmetics downwards. Retailers were calling on Natura to offer more favourable terms or, as one customer commented, '...there are plenty of other suppliers we can do business with'.

It was against this background of gathering gloom that Wasim called a full-day meeting of Natura's board of directors. He had managed the company in a paternalistic manner and during the years of growth and prosperity this approach had caused little controversy. The workforce trusted him and he was used to having his way on major decisions.

Wasim started by outlining the company's present situation, drawing attention to the decline in operating profits — nearly 10% over the past 2 years. 'We have been forced to reduce prices at a time when minimum wage legislation has forced up our wage costs. The performance of our workforce is a major concern to me, particularly as unemployment has fallen and employees have found it easier to find alternative work. Our shop-floor employees are simply not performing sufficiently well, in view of the increasing competitiveness of the market for natural cosmetics. I think they have underachieved in recent years.'

Wasim had surprised the Board by making the following proposals:
(1) The factory in Gloucester should be closed and Natura's production in Barnsley scaled down.
(2) Workers should be redeployed wherever possible to factories in Birmingham and Stockport or be offered voluntary redundancy packages. In spite of this, compulsory redundancies would almost certainly be necessary.

(3) Negotiations to purchase a large factory in western Poland are well advanced. This has the capacity to supply customers in the UK and provide an opportunity to break into the prosperous European markets.

(4) Natura will mount a major marketing campaign to persuade European retailers to stock the full range of the company's products.

(5) Natura's product range is inadequate for the European market. Funds will be invested in developing a new range of cosmetics designed for European markets. A figure of £72.4 million has been included in the budget for the next financial year to fund the necessary research and development.

(6) A new workforce plan will be presented to next month's Board meeting, once the company's future need for employees becomes clearer.

Wasim's proposals sparked a furious debate amongst the members of the board of directors, much of which was highly critical of the plans. David Chell, a worker director, expressed his astonishment at the plans. 'In the past you have always consulted us about major changes, even if you have taken the final decision. But this is all news to me. I thought you were a fair leader and a good communicator. You appear to have adopted a much harder approach to human resource management. Why haven't you consulted with us?'

Wasim acknowledged that his approach to workforce planning had changed, but argued that this was inevitable in the circumstances. 'Our future is bright, but we must be proactive and act in advance of real difficulties. Our workforce is a vital competitive weapon and tough decisions are essential in this respect. I'm convinced that in a few years' time you'll all be grateful for this plan.'

Other directors were concerned about the risk inherent in a strategy which placed great reliance on moving part of the business overseas. There was some discussion about the greater complexity of taking international location decisions. Some directors had doubts about the wisdom of moving part of the business to Poland and becoming a multinational. One commented that the cost advantages would probably be more than offset by non-financial factors. She continued: 'Any financial advantages from moving to Poland will be more than offset by the money you are proposing to invest in research and development. We would be better advised to remain in the UK and spend the money on the workforce and improving productivity — that is a more immediate need.'

Appendix A Figures for shop-floor workers in Natura's UK factories

Year	Labour turnover %	Wage costs (hourly rate, £)	Absenteeism %	Productivity index
1996	4.1	3.33	2.9	100
1997	4.9	3.58	3.3	101
1998	4.9	3.69	4.4	96
1999	6.0	3.98	4.7	98
2000	6.5	4.22	4.9	101
2001	6.6	4.44	4.8	103

(1) (a) Why might decisions regarding international location be more complex
than location decisions within a country? (6 marks)

(b) Discuss the case for and against Natura moving part of its production
to Poland. (14 marks)

(2) Discuss the factors Natura should consider before deciding whether to invest
over £72 million in a programme of research and development. (20 marks)

(3) (a) Do you think Wasim is justified in expressing concern over the
performance of Natura's workforce in the years to 2001? (10 marks)

(b) Wasim believes that his workforce has underachieved over recent years.
To what extent is Wasim himself responsible for this? (10 marks)

(4) (a) Explain how good communication might contribute to the successful
implementation of Wasim's plans. (6 marks)

(b) To what extent was Wasim's change in approach to workforce planning
'inevitable' in view of the declining competitiveness of Natura? (14 marks)

Total: 80 marks

■ ■ ■

Answer to question 3: candidate A

(1) (a) Decisions involving international location are more complex because they are
affected by exchange rates. Natura might find that its costs increase in Poland
because of a change in the value of the Polish currency. This may make financial
planning more risky.

Locating overseas involves different legislation. It is not easy for foreigners to
understand the detail of Polish business legislation, even though it may be less
comprehensive than that of the UK. It is possible to hire consultants to offer advice
on such matters, but this advice may be inaccurate and Natura's directors would
not know this.

🖉 This is a confident and effective start. Candidate A shows a good understanding
of the relevant subject matter and has resisted the temptation to spend too long
on this relatively 'easy' topic. Even though the question did not directly refer to
Natura, it is always good practice to relate answers to the case study.

(b) There are obvious cost advantages of moving to Poland as mentioned in the
case study. Polish workers' wages are likely to be much lower than those paid in
the UK and this will have a major impact on the costs of production and the
efficiency of the firm. Employment legislation is also likely to be less extensive,
allowing the firm to operate working practices that are illegal in the UK. For
example, health and safety legislation may be weak, reducing the need for expenditure on non-productive personnel such as safety officers. Costs of renting or
purchasing property will probably be significantly less, further contributing to lower
costs of production and competitiveness.

But there are qualitative factors to take into account too. Will the Polish workforce possess the necessary skills to carry out the production line work for Natura? A cheaper workforce will be of little benefit if they are much less productive, meaning that Natura's unit costs rise rather than fall. Communications problems will almost certainly affect operations, especially in the short-term while workers are becoming familiar with their new duties. The employment of bilingual managers for the Polish plant may assist in overcoming this difficulty, but will add to production costs.

Whether the proposed move to Poland will reduce costs may depend upon the level of skills required by Natura's production line employees. If the workers require few skills, training costs are reduced and the language barrier becomes less problematic. Given the wage rates recorded in Appendix A, it appears unlikely that Natura employs highly skilled employees and so the move to Poland might be worthwhile.

> This is another good answer. Candidate A has not been too ambitious in the answer's scope in response to a very broad question. The structure is exemplary, offering arguments for and against the proposed location, always relating the response to the scenario in the case study. The evaluation is very thoughtful and is a natural development of the earlier analysis. Once again candidate A makes very effective use of the information given in the case study.

(2) The financial aspects of investing over £72 million are obviously important. The company is proposing this investment against a background of declining profits. The company's profits have fallen significantly at a time when the economy was booming and demand for products such as cosmetics would probably have been rising. Therefore it may have to borrow money; this could be expensive and risky if sales and profits continue to decline. The company would be advised to use techniques such as the average rate of return to appraise this investment and to compare it with any alternative that might exist.

The company needs to take into account the competitive position within the market. Increasing numbers of firms are appearing and Natura's unique selling point is declining in importance. The company can no longer use this as a reason to charge higher prices. Therefore it needs to differentiate itself in some other way. Producing an extended range of products that may be different in some way from those already on the market might be a good move in the circumstances. In particular, the company will have to prepare to meet the differing demands of consumers in other European countries.

An obvious factor to take into account is the views of retailers and consumers. Why are Natura's products less popular than in the past? Discovering the probable cause of declining popularity would be a logical first step along the road to resolving it. Wasim seems to have simply decided that R&D is the answer and is determined to go ahead. More thought and some research might be advisable. It would also be useful to carry out some internal research to assess existing products and identify, for example, those that may be nearing the end of their product life cycles.

3

question

🖉 Candidate A has compiled three sound arguments concerning factors that Natura may take into account as part of the investment decision. These are clearly explained and closely linked into the scenario. However, the candidate has not attempted to evaluate the answers. This question is not two-sided and does not offer the opportunity to make a judgement between two arguments. Evaluating this type of question requires a different approach. The candidate could have judged which was the most important factor affecting the decision and have justified that choice. This would have made this into a high-quality answer.

(3) (a) The most important data relate to productivity. By 2001 the efficiency of Natura's workforce had only improved by 3% in comparison with 1996. This probably means that the company will have slipped behind in comparison with its competitors. In part this might explain the increasing difficulty Natura has had in matching the prices charged by rivals. The only slight encouragement is that there has been an improvement since 1999 over which period wages have also risen more quickly.

Labour turnover is also quite high and has increased through the period. In the 6 years covered by the data, Natura will have 'lost' approximately one-third of its workforce. This commits the company to substantial costs for recruitment, selection and training each year whilst contributing to a less experienced workforce. On the other hand, some new employees each year is a healthy sign, bringing new ideas and enthusiasm into Natura's workforce.

🖉 This answer is sound, though it could have been developed further. The basic structure is fine. Candidate A has picked out two important themes and has explained the positive and negative implications of the data. The temptation to attempt to comment on all the figures is resisted. About 10 minutes was available to plan and write this answer, so it is important to be selective.

(b) Wasim is clearly dissatisfied with his workforce, but much of the responsibility is his. He has led his employees in a paternalistic manner, probably giving little authority to those lower down the hierarchy. In these circumstances, productivity levels are unlikely to be high.

Natura's pay rates are also low. In 1999 the company had to increase rates to ensure workers received the minimum wage. Pay may not be a major motivator, but it is important to prevent dissatisfaction amongst workers. The labour turnover figures do suggest some level of unhappiness and this may be due to low levels of pay.

The amount of training received by employees is an important factor. More training should improve the level of output and make customers more satisfied. It may improve both the quality and quantity of production.

There are other factors that might have affected the achievements of the workforce beyond the control of Wasim. The level of education received by employees will be important, as will the infrastructure available locally.

🖉 The quality of this answer deteriorates as it progresses. The first two paragraphs argue why Wasim should take responsibility for the relatively poor performance of the workforce. Candidate A develops thoughts demonstrating an ability to analyse. After this the answer loses direction and the quality declines. A list of relevant arguments is offered with no development.

(4) (a) Wasim is a paternalistic manager and it may be that much of his communication is downward. If he is to avoid a major industrial dispute he needs to talk to the workforce and possibly to involve them in the decision-making process to some degree. If he doesn't consult properly, then his plans may be delayed or ruined by industrial action. Another point is that it will be much more difficult to communicate with a factory in Poland. Clearly there will be a language barrier. Unless this is overcome, the expected decrease in costs might not occur.

🖉 This is a sound answer, even if it is a little brief. Candidate A identifies some good points and focuses on communication as an element of leadership style. This demonstrates an effective combination of knowledge and the skills of application and analysis.

(b) Wasim was correct when he argued that the company needed to take some action. It is clear that the company is becoming less competitive against rival businesses. To seek to reduce costs by relocating some of the company's operations is one method of improving competitiveness. Even if workers are not more productive, lower wages are more than likely to compensate for this. This move will allow Natura to reduce its costs of production and to charge lower prices to retailers whilst maintaining profit margins.

But there were many other methods by which Wasim could have enhanced the competitiveness of his business. He could have sought to empower the labour force and, by giving them more interesting roles and greater authority and control over their working lives, he could have improved productivity and quality. This would have required substantial investment and a change in philosophy if it were to succeed. Furthermore, competitiveness is not entirely dependent upon the workforce: more investment in technology may have achieved the desired effect.

It is possible to argue that it was not inevitable that a harder approach to HRM was 'inevitable' in view of the alternative means of improving competitiveness. However, I think that it was inevitable given Wasim's leadership style and views on employees. As a paternalistic leader he was likely to adopt a harder approach and, under pressure, it was perhaps inevitable that Wasim would revert to type.

🖉 This is a high-quality final response to the case study. Candidate A presented analysis on both sides of the argument before writing an excellent concluding paragraph. It is worth reading this carefully. The candidate reaches a cogently argued judgement, rooted in the context of the case, and exhibits a clear understanding of Wasim's leadership style and its implications.

🖉 **In spite of some variation in quality, this is an excellent set of answers and would be worthy of a grade A overall.**

■ ■ ■

question 3

Answer to question 3: candidate B

(1) (a) Decisions over international location might be more complex for many reasons. The company will have to deal with different cultures and languages and will face strange legal systems and perhaps more red tape.

The company might find it more difficult to get the information it needs when it doesn't have the necessary contacts. The company might even find opposition from some people overseas. There are also financial problems — the company might lose out to changing exchange rates, or tariffs and quotas might cause problems for the firm. For all of these reasons Natura will need to think extra carefully about locating overseas.

> ✍ This is a content-heavy answer and one that is not entirely appropriate as an answer to A2 questions. Candidate B has identified many reasons that may make decisions regarding international location more complicated. However, the candidate has failed to develop an answer to explain *why* these factors make the decision more complex. The answer was too ambitious in its scope.

(b) The company will gain many benefits from moving some of its production to Poland. Firstly, if the firm intends to export to Europe, opening a factory in western Poland will make this ideal for the markets of central Europe. A number of countries, such as Poland and Hungary, are joining the EU so this is a good location for the future. The costs of running a factory in Poland are also likely to be much cheaper with all sorts of costs being lower than they would be in England. This will help Natura to be more price competitive in the UK and the rest of Europe.

But this decision needs careful thought, as there are a number of potential problems. Communications within Poland may not be as good as in Western Europe, meaning transporting materials and finished products is more expensive and slower than the firm might want. The firm might also encounter difficulties, particularly in the short-term, as the factory experiences teething problems. It may be that they are unable to fulfil orders on time or of suitable quality, leaving customers dissatisfied.

Wasim appears to have taken the decision to relocate to Poland for cost reasons. This might, however, prove to be a false economy. Natura's customers purchase its products for a variety of reasons: they do not simply select the cheapest product available. Retail outlets will expect quality products delivered on time and if the Polish factory cannot achieve this, then having a price advantage may be of little value.

> ✍ There is much to admire in this answer. Candidate B has structured the answer well, considering both sides of the issue before composing a thoughtful and well-judged evaluation. The weakness is that the candidate doesn't really develop sufficient analysis in the first two paragraphs. Candidate B identifies a number of good points but instead of expanding them in the context of the case, moves on to offer another reason.

(2) Natura is considering making a huge investment of £72 million to research and introduce a range of new cosmetics for the European market. This will allow the company to compete effectively against foreign producers and to meet the needs of consumers in countries such as France and Germany. This will also help to boost the company's sales in Britain.

The company might want to consider whether the range of products it is currently selling are in the final stages of their life cycles. If this is the case, with competitors bringing newer cosmetics onto the market, perhaps using new ingredients, then there is a stronger case for Natura to spend this amount of money on R&D. However, if its products are still selling fairly well this may not be necessary. It seems from the case that Natura is struggling in terms of price; there is no suggestion that the products themselves are becoming less popular.

However, the best time for Natura to research new products is when its existing cosmetics are selling well. If it leaves the decision until sales are declining as the products enter the final stage of their life cycles, then there will probably be insufficient time to bring new products onto the market before revenues fall seriously.

Natura is planning to sell its cosmetics to European consumers. This is a new market for the company and it will be essential to conduct market research to find out what European consumers want and how Europe differs from the UK market. Natura may already have carried out market research to establish that a market exists for its cosmetics. The results of the research will form the basis for market research. This market-orientated approach should help to ensure that the R&D ultimately proves successful.

> ✐ This does not begin well. Candidate B is probably still thinking about the answer when writing the first paragraph. This paragraph does not answer the question and is mainly a rewrite of information from the case. It is better to think a little more and to ensure that all of an answer is relevant. The remaining paragraphs are fair, as candidate B explains factors that Natura may consider, though at times the question is not directly addressed. It is also disappointing that there is no conclusion and no evaluation in this response.

(3) (a) Wasim is right to be worried about the figures on the performance of Natura's workforce. The figure for labour turnover is high and it gets worse over time, rising from 4.1% in 1996 to 6.0% in 1999 and 6.6% in 2001. The rate at which it increases is slowing as time passes.

Hourly wage costs have gone up by one-third between 1996 and 2001. Natura was paying £3.33 in 1996 and this had risen to £4.44 by 2001 — a big increase. Absenteeism has also risen from 2.9% in 1996 to 4.8% by the end of the period. This would be a major cause of worry for Wasim. The most worrying figures, however, are those relating to productivity. The company looks little better off in 2001 than it was in 1996, at a time when competitors may have increased productivity, increasing their share of the market.

e This is not a strong answer. Candidate B has fallen into the old trap of describing the data rather than interpreting them. This question required analysis of the data and consideration of whether they indicated a poor performance by Natura's employees.

(b) Ultimately Wasim is responsible for the performance of everyone in the company as he is the chief executive. Thus if the shop-floor employees have not succeeded, it is the responsibility of Wasim. A leader sets the objectives for the business, has a major say in recruiting the staff and will set out the personnel policies that the business pursues.

The leader also develops the structure of the organisation, deciding on the levels of hierarchy, the channels for communication and the span of control that managers have. The leader will decide whether the organisation is delayered and the amount of responsibility given to junior workers. Most importantly, the leader will shape the culture of the business and this will influence the performance of the employees in many ways. In a task culture, employees might show initiative and solve problems without too much guidance from managers. A leader encouraging this sort of culture can influence the performance of the workforce.

e Candidate B begins the answer with a conclusion — a better approach would have been to present the evidence before making any sort of judgement. Overall, this is another unimpressive response. Candidate B has not made any use of the information in the case study. It is an entirely theoretical response, with only a token reference to Wasim in the first paragraph. There was a lot of information in the text on which to base an argument about the influence of Wasim's leadership, but this has been ignored.

(4) (a) Communication is the exchange of ideas or information. Communication can take several forms including talking in meetings, writing memos and letters, and using IT such as e-mail.

Opening a factory in Poland means that the company will have to make more use of technology to achieve its aim of competing more effectively. E-mail could be used to send orders to the factory instantly and to order supplies for the new factory.

It may be helpful if the company trains some of its employees to speak Polish. This might avoid a number of language problems that are likely to occur.

e This is a brief response that does not really answer the question. Candidate B defines communication and gives examples, but then focuses on how to improve communication rather than explaining why good communication might be important.

(b) Natura appears to be losing out to competitors and suffering because other companies are setting lower prices. Wasim was under pressure to introduce policies to respond to this loss of price competitiveness. In this way change was inevitable, but not necessarily the change that was suggested and which upset the board of directors.

Wasim could have considered offering much more training to Natura's employees in the hope of improving productivity. Training may give shop-floor workers the skills to work more effectively and to avoid making errors and producing substandard cosmetics. Training may also motivate employees as they feel more valued and can perhaps take on a wider range of duties on the production line. In fact, training might allow workers to become multi-skilled, switching between different tasks with few problems and assisting the continuity of production.

Competitiveness can be enhanced through a range of other techniques, such as carrying out a merger or taking over a rival company. Increasing the scale of production in this way can be a very effective means of reducing costs of production as a consequence of economies of scale. Given Natura's desire to break into the European market, this might be the best way for the company to improve its competitiveness and to gain some insight into the European market and the different types of consumers. It would also provide a fairly quick means of improving competitiveness.

This response contains a number of good elements. Candidate B identifies several ways in which the company could improve its competitiveness without adopting the approach favoured by Wasim. However, the answer loses its focus after an interesting opening paragraph. Although the suggestions are perfectly reasonable, the answer needed to concentrate on the inevitability, or otherwise, of Wasim's proposal in the circumstances.

Candidate B's factual knowledge and analytical skills would have been sufficient to achieve a sound pass, possibly grade E or D, but would have secured relatively few of the marks available for the skills of application and evaluation.

An integrated case study

Applegate Farms Ltd

'Devon is famous for food and farming: Devon cream teas, cider, pork chops and butter, cows grazing contentedly. Its all idyllic stuff, I know, but it is an image on which we can build a marketing campaign.' Rick Jackman paused and looked around the table. His colleagues were interested and Rick's enthusiasm for his plans grew.

Rick was making a presentation to his fellow directors, outlining a new venture for Applegate Farms Ltd. The company owns and operates 37 farms across Devon covering more than 30,000 acres. In spite of the pressures on farming (for example, the foot and mouth crisis in 2001) the company had returned a steady profit over the last 10 years. However, the core of Rick's presentation was that the return on capital generated by the company was not satisfactory. 'We could increase our profitability if we look to sell a high proportion of our own products under our farm-assured label. At the moment the supermarkets are making a lot of profit that could be ours, if only we take the plunge. We must not abandon our long-term objective of growth, but increasing profitability is also important.'

Having captured the attention of the other directors, Rick expanded his ideas. 'We open a chain of 40 farm shops in Devon, Dorset and Somerset. These outlets (a mixture of a farm-gate shop and a small supermarket) should stock all of our produce. We could sell meat, cheese, fruit and vegetables as well as beer and cider. The emphasis should be on quality and fresh wholesome foods. This will allow premium pricing. The market for food is changing and consumers want to be assured that what they are eating is safe. Knowing where it comes from helps.'

The finance director supported Rick's plans, but sounded a note of caution. She warned that the company would need to raise £16 million to open the shops, establish a distribution network and provide working capital for the new enterprise. 'Our gearing position makes it difficult for us to raise large amounts of capital easily. We need to consider the financial aspect of this situation carefully before taking the plunge. Certainly we should consider diverse methods of raising the finance needed, including government agencies.'

Rick acknowledged the importance of the monetary issues surrounding the proposal. He identified two steps that were essential to strengthen the company's financial position. 'Firstly, the company should hire business consultants to help plan the process and to permit the use of decision-making techniques. Critical path analysis, for example, could offer many advantages and prove cost-effective. The shops must be operational as quickly as possible, and definitely before July (allowing 10 months). Being able to sell to the tourist market is essential to boost initial sales revenue. CPA will assist in coordinating the leasing of property, arranging for storage and distribution, developing a marketing campaign and recruiting staff. Secondly, the company should utilise information technology to the fullest possible extent in planning the development of the farm shops. Use of IT could also improve the efficiency of the farm shop operation once it is established, in particular by minimising costs.'

Rick had one more element of his proposal to reveal. 'To operate 40 shops will require an enormous increase in staff and considerable retailing expertise. None of us has that experience and I am nervous at the prospect of hiring a large number of new staff. We would need in excess of 200 staff and the process of recruitment and selection alone would take a huge amount of time. I am very attracted by the idea of subcontracting the operation of the farm shops to another company, rather than recruiting our own full-time staff. There are considerable financial and non-financial benefits in this approach and I have spoken to another company, South West Enterprises, and they are interested in negotiating a deal.'

Rick looked around the room. 'We have come a long way together, but this represents another big step. We must take some important decisions.'

Appendix A Financial statements for Applegate Farms Ltd

Applegate Farms Ltd — balance sheet as at 30 September		
	2002	2001
	(£000s)	(£000s)
Fixed assets	74,845	81,232
Current assets		
Stock	18,904	19,348
Debtors and cash	1,104	1,206
Less current liabilities	(19,577)	(22,662)
Net assets employed	75,276	79,124
Long-term liabilities	33,717	36,615
Shareholders' funds	41,559	42,509
Capital employed	75,276	79,124

Applegate Farms Ltd — extracts from profit and loss accounts		
	2002	2001
	(£000s)	(£000s)
Turnover	81,944	86,252
Cost of sales	54,375	55,413
Gross profit	27,569	30,839
Expenses	16,399	19,804
Operating profit	11,170	11,035

question

(1) (a) Examine the difficulties Applegate Farms might encounter when
forecasting the expected levels of sales from its farm shops. (8 marks)

(b) Applegate Farms has little direct competition for its new farm shops.
Discuss the marketing strategy the firm might employ in these
circumstances. (12 marks)

(2) (a) The finance director is concerned about the company's working capital
position if it decides to open the farm shops. How might Applegate Farms
improve its position with regard to working capital? (10 marks)

(b) How useful might Applegate's financial statements be to someone
considering investing in the company's expansion programme? (10 marks)

(3) (a) Assess the ways in which Applegate Farms might use information
technology in the operation of its farm shops. (8 marks)

(b) Rick Jackman has proposed that the company uses critical path analysis
to assist in completing the project as quickly as possible. Evaluate whether
critical path analysis is likely to be of value in these circumstances. (12 marks)

(4) Discuss the case for and against Applegate Farms subcontracting the
operation of its farm shops to South West Enterprises. (20 marks)

Total: 80 marks

■ ■ ■

Answer to question 4: candidate A

(1) (a) Applegate Farms could face a lot of problems when attempting to forecast its
sales from the farm shops. Its market is potentially enormous and probably very
varied — people of all ages, income levels and social classes might buy food in
the farm shops. This makes it difficult to find out consumer views with accuracy
without spending huge amounts of money on market research. The firm would
have to take a big sample of people to get an accurate figure and this might take
time as well. Given that Rick Jackman wants to have the shops operational within
10 months, time is short. Therefore producing accurate data in this situation might
be difficult.

Applegate Farms has no experience of retailing and has not managed shops before.
Therefore the company cannot use past trading figures to indicate future sales.
Extrapolation will not be possible. Rick Jackman has said that there are no similar
enterprises that they might be able to analyse to give some indication of future
sales. Consequently, any forecast is more likely to be a stab in the dark and perhaps
not very accurate.

    This is a good-quality answer of appropriate length. Candidate A has presented
it in two paragraphs and this structure has encouraged the full development of
the arguments. However, its major strength is that it makes extensive and effective use of the information in the case study to construct the answer. This has
helped to ensure that marks are gained for application. Using the prompts in the
case in this way is helpful in putting together relevant arguments.

(b) A marketing strategy is the means by which an organisation intends to attain its marketing objectives. It is a long-term plan for marketing activities that also takes into account the resources available to the business and the actions of rival firms.

Applegate Farms' marketing strategy will be easier to design and implement because of the absence of direct competitors. The major influences on the company's plans will be the resources it has available and its overall objectives. Applegate's financial position is not strong and it needs to improve profitability. It is also looking to achieve long-term growth. This is perfectly possible and the company can use its marketing strategy to achieve both.

Opening the farm shops with little competition means that the company can charge relatively high prices. Rick mentions the possibility of premium pricing. This will help the company to gain more profit and will help improve the financial position.

The company plans to open 40 farm shops. The marketing strategy will have to support this by informing the public of the opening of the shops and by including essential promotional activities to increase consumer awareness. The emphasis could be on the nature of the products it is selling and how these might differ from those sold in ordinary supermarkets such as Tesco.

> Candidate A has written a sound answer here, but one which does not really fulfil its early promise. It starts well by explaining clearly what a marketing strategy is, ensuring that any marks available for subject knowledge are gained. The paragraph on the influences on marketing strategies is interesting, though the best use of this was not made in later paragraphs. The final two paragraphs are underdeveloped. In particular, it would have been interesting to consider the issue of pricing in more detail. Candidate A presumably thinks demand for Applegate Farms' produce is price inelastic. Is this likely to be true? If so, why? Some conclusion offering evaluation would have improved the quality of this response.

(2) (a) Applegate Farms does not have much working capital. Using the formula, working capital = current assets – current liabilities, we can see that in 2001 the company had a negative working capital figure of over £2 million. This means that it is essential that the company takes action if it is to grow.

A good approach would be to reduce the business's need for working capital. It is vital that the company operates strict credit control throughout its organisation, but particularly in its new enterprise to ensure that cash enters the business promptly and regularly. This will reduce short-term borrowing and the need for working capital.

The company might also seek to borrow long term to improve its working capital position. The company's gearing position is sound and this action would be possible. It is important that the firm plans to avoid a liquidity crisis occurring.

question

One point in Applegate Farms' favour is that its customers will mainly pay cash, meaning that the firm will not have to await payment. Credit sales might be fairly unusual in this position.

> 🖉 This is a fair attempt at answering a tricky question. The candidate recognises the importance to Applegate Farms of reducing its working capital requirements, though this line of argument could have been developed further. Candidate A offers some advice on how the company might improve its working capital situation. The final paragraph represents good understanding of working capital in the context of the question. Retailers can manage with low liquidity levels.

(b) The accounts give a clear picture of the company's financial performance to date and help potential lenders to assess the strength of the business and the ability of the management team. They also help lenders to make an assessment of the current financial position of the business. In particular, they could view the cash position of the business and its gearing ratio in order to make a judgement about the ability of the business to repay any loans made to it.

But much of this project is not shown in the accounts. The risk of the project needs to be assessed. If it is not regarded as being a high risk, investors might put money into Applegate Farms in spite of its low return on capital. The degree of risk will also be shaped by the degree of competition existing in the market. If there is not a great deal, then the investment will look attractive, irrespective of the business's financial state. Risk will be a major influence on the decisions of potential investors, and this is only partially shown by Applegate's accounts.

The accounts provide a mainly historical view of Applegate. More information is required to make a judgement as to the potential risks and benefits that might be gained from investing in the firm. However, the fact that the accounts have to be presented in a standard format makes comparisons with other companies easier.

> 🖉 This is a well-structured answer to the question. Candidate A appreciates the need to present arguments for and against the use of financial statements in assessing the value of the investment opportunity offered by the farm shops idea. However, no use is made of the data within the financial statements — a serious omission. The final paragraph offers an overall judgement, though this could, perhaps, have been developed further with more evidence supporting the candidate's point of view.

(3) (a) There are a number of ways in which Applegate might use IT in its new venture. IT could be used to place orders for products from each of the farm shops. Using IT in this way offers a number of benefits. The company would find that it did not need to hold as many stocks. This would reduce costs as the firm would not require as much storage space, particularly cold storage for food which might be perishable. The firm might be able to use just-in-time systems and this would allow storage facilities to be almost eliminated.

It offers other benefits too. Applegate could allow customers to purchase using the internet and then provide a delivery service. This might make the service attractive to wealthier customers who have busy jobs that don't allow time for shopping, but who want to purchase the types of foods supplied by Applegate Farms. This might be a point that the company could use in its advertising, providing it with a unique selling point.

This answer reads well and identifies two relevant ways in which Applegate Farms might use IT in its new venture. However, the answer is not balanced — it considers the benefits of using IT in the ways suggested without examining any potential disadvantages. The answer should explore and weigh up the possible drawbacks as well.

(b) Critical path analysis is a means of representing complex issues and decisions on a diagram. The technique allows managers to identify activities that are completed on time, reducing costs and assisting in making effective decisions.

CPA would assist the business in planning the opening of the farm shops and assist in helping the business to meet its 10 month deadline. The technique would assist the firm in assessing the activities that must be completed, identify those that can be completed simultaneously and thereby reduce the amount of time taken for the entire project. CPA offers other advantages to Applegate. The technique may help the firm to use the minimum possible amount of resources in planning and introducing the new farm shops. For example, staff overseeing the project may be able to switch from one activity to another and complete a series of tasks, so reducing the expenses on wages.

But the opening of 40 farm shops is an immensely complex activity and it is unlikely that this could be drawn on a network easily. If it was it may create a huge network that can only be displayed and interpreted by computers. Given that Applegate's management team is obviously inexperienced in using critical path analysis, starting with such a complicated network might be unsuccessful.

For the use of critical path analysis to be successful for Applegate Farms in implementing its plan for farm shops, other aspects of successful management would have to be in place. CPA can help good managers manage effectively, but it will not cure underlying problems such as poor marketing and ineffectual personnel management. CPA is more likely to help Applegate if appropriate staff are involved in the decisions and have some authority delegated to them — in this way it is more likely that the plan set out in the network will become reality.

This is an excellent answer to a challenging question. Candidate A has demonstrated understanding of critical path analysis at the outset and through the analysis offered. This sets out the two sides of the argument, continually relating it to the circumstances of Applegate Farms. Finally, a well-judged evaluation is given in the last paragraph.

(4) Rick included the suggestion that another company should operate the new farm shops on behalf of Applegate in his proposal. Applegate Farms could benefit in a number of ways from subcontracting the operation of the business to South West Enterprises. The company would be spared the cost and risk of recruiting employees to run a business about which Applegate's managers have little knowledge. Recruiting employees to manage and staff 40 farm shops would take a considerable amount of time and cost — a substantial sum in terms of advertising and staff time. The company may even have to pay for consultants to appoint the more senior employees (shop managers or managers of groups of shops, for example). Applegate would also avoid some additional costs, such as training, that may be essential before the shops can be opened. The process of subcontracting would significantly reduce the initial costs of the scheme and reduce the difficulties of entering a new business.

On the other hand, Applegate would face potential problems if it went ahead with its decision to subcontract the operation of its new farm shops. Applegate would not have the degree of control over this element of its business that it would have if it ran the retail business itself. The company might find that the quality of service is not of the standard that is expected. This might detract from Applegate's image as a supplier of wholesome and safe food and result in the business achieving lower sales than forecast. Communication may be more difficult if Applegate is made up of two separate businesses with different management teams, possibly different management information systems and different cultures. Poor communications could be a major drawback, especially if techniques such as just-in-time are used.

Subcontracting the operation of the farm shops would assist Applegate in the short term, reducing its costs and probably the risk of starting this new venture. But in the long term it could prove expensive as South West Enterprises would want a share of the profits and may not reach the standards desired by Applegate. Applegate should consider whether subcontracting would help it to achieve growth and increased profitability in the long term.

✑ This is another strong answer, combining subject knowledge and examination skills very effectively. A particularly good feature is the regular use of the case study as a basis for the answer. The candidate has drawn on information in the text and uses it in constructing arguments on both sides.

✑ **Candidate A would gain credit for using the material presented in the case study as an integral part of the answer. Although the candidate occasionally loses sight of the question, the combination of thorough subject knowledge and first-class examination skills means that this set of answers is worthy of a grade A.**

■ ■ ■

Answer to question 4: candidate B

(1) (a) Applegate is selling products that are seasonal. It will find that its demand will vary throughout the year, selling more fruit in the warm months for example. This will be difficult to predict and will mean that the company's sales forecasts are more likely to be wrong.

The firm does not know how other firms might respond. Supermarkets like Somerfield might start to sell 'farm fresh' foods in certain parts of its super-markets. These could be set up pretty quickly once Applegate Farms Ltd's plans become known and may steal a lot of sales from the new farm shops. Applegate might also base sales forecasts on its first few weeks of trading when sales are high as people investigate the business. Actual sales might be lower in later weeks.

✐ This answer contains some good points but looks as if it was written without much forethought or planning. The first paragraph is not well argued. It is not the demand for Applegate's products that will be seasonal; rather it is the supply. The second paragraph is better, but the arguments could have been developed further, though the candidate did try to relate them to the scenario.

(b) The firm could benefit in a number of ways from having no direct competition at the outset of its venture:

- Consumers might be interested in trying out what they see as a new service and this might mean that sales are much higher than initially expected, although these may fall after a few months once the initial popularity of the farm shops has worn off.
- It might be able to charge higher prices because consumers cannot buy the products from anywhere else. This will make the company more profitable as it gets more profits on each sale.
- The firm will not have to spend as much on advertising as it might if there was a direct competitor for its products. This will help to reduce costs and improve its profitability, especially in the first few months.
- Being the first on the market might help to establish it as the best in the eyes of the consumers. Again, this will help sales.

✐ This is a very disappointing answer. Candidate B does not appear to have much, if any, knowledge about marketing strategy — the question is interpreted generally, only focusing on the benefits of facing little direct competition. The use of bullet points makes it unlikely that any development will take place. This makes it virtually impossible to earn analysis marks. The other major shortcoming of this answer is that candidate B has not related the response to the scenario at any point. It could refer to any business in any circumstances.

(2) (a) Working capital is the cash needed by a business to pay for its day-to-day expenses. It might be used to pay wages and to pay for raw materials and fuel. If Applegate Farms expands, then it is likely to need more working capital to run its

question

new venture. The farm's working capital is its current assets less its current liabilities. This can be read from Applegate Farms' balance sheet.

It might get more working capital if it borrows money from the bank. This is important to ensure that the company does not get a reputation for being a slow payer and upsetting suppliers, meaning that they may not be happy to trade with the company.

> Candidate B has a fair knowledge of working capital and is able to define it and explain how it might be calculated. However, the candidate is unable to discuss how a firm's working capital position might be improved, particularly in the context of this question. This answer demonstrates a weakness in higher-order skills, especially application and analysis.

(b) Published accounts can be very helpful in reaching a decision on how to raise capital for capital investment. This is true of Applegate too. The company can use its accounts to support an application to a bank for a loan. Applegate could use this information to persuade a bank manager that the company has the resources to pay back a bank loan and to show that it is investing some money from retained profits. This will make a stronger case for the business and may mean that it is not charged a really high rate of interest, as it is not seen to be a risk.

The accounts may also give a history of the firm's financial performance. It is fairly common for firms to give 5–year summaries of their financial performance in their annual report and accounts. This means that individuals and firms considering putting money into the business can see how the business has performed over time, helping to give a view of the trend. So long as the trend is improving, the accounts are likely to prove useful.

> Candidate B has made a fairly common error in answering this question. The question is not interpreted fully and the answer is written to support a narrow construction, ignoring the possibility of putting an alternative point of view. Given this error, it was extremely unlikely that any evaluation would be offered. A question that asks 'How useful...?' is not just looking for an answer that shows how useful a factor is; it should also include comments on why the factor might not be useful, and then draw an overall conclusion on its usefulness.

(3) (a) Applegate Farms Ltd could use IT in lots of ways in its farm shops. Some ways include the following:
- IT could be used to communicate between the shops and head office and the farms. This might be best using e-mail.
- IT could also be used to design posters and other publicity materials in the shops to help advertise the business.
- Another use of IT might be for storing records of the business, so as to save time and space.
- It could help to print out graphs and charts showing the performance of individual shops, which would help managers.

• It would be useful for recording customers' details, making it easy to write to them in the future.

🖉 Once again, this is disappointing. Candidate B has simply shown some knowledge of the ways in which IT may be used in a business. This is not related properly to the circumstances of Applegate Farms and the use of bullet points means that an analysis is not offered. Candidate B appears to be unaware of the meaning of the command words (or verbs) in the question. In this case the command word is 'assess', inviting a two-sided response and some evaluation. Unfortunately, much of this is lacking.

(b) Critical path analysis is a system used to help managers to make decisions on difficult subjects. It is based on diagrams that have lines showing activities and circles — or nodes — representing the start and finish of the activities. By calculating earliest start times and latest finish times, it is possible to find out the critical path — that is the way to conduct the activity in the shortest possible time. Any delays on this critical path will delay the whole activity.

Critical path analysis is an important part of business decision-making and charts can be drawn quickly on computers. Computers can also show complex networks and can construct them in seconds.

Critical path analysis will help Applegate to plan the process of opening 40 farm shops as quickly as possible. This will help the company to avoid expensive delays and help to ensure that it meets the deadline of next summer. Critical path analysis will also help the company to get the right resources at the right time. So when it needs to fit out the shops, it will have the resources and staff available. Workers will not stand idle with nothing to do.

But critical path analysis is complicated and the managers at Applegate may not know anything about it and have to go on training courses. Even then they may not be very good at it.

🖉 Candidate B has a fair knowledge of critical path analysis, and it is fine to provide a definition. However, too much time has been spent describing the technique. In the latter stages, the answer begins to consider the advantages and disadvantages of CPA, and makes some attempt to link it to the scenario. However, this is too little, too late and evaluation has not been attempted.

(4) Subcontracting means that a firm asks another firm to carry out part of its work for it. Applegate is planning to ask South West Enterprises to run the farm shops for it. This will help the company to get the farm shops up and running quickly as it doesn't have to hire lots of employees and appoint managers. It can just say to the other company that it wants to run the shops from a certain date.

Applegate will also know how much it is going to cost from the outset as South West will charge a fee for its work, making it easier for the company to budget.

But there are some drawbacks too:
- loss of control of the new business
- Applegate employees become demotivated because they lose the chance of promotion
- more expensive than paying own staff
- breakdown of communication
- sorry, ran out of time...

Candidate B has not managed time well and could not complete this answer. In these circumstances it is not a good idea to use bullet points as this means that no marks for application or analysis are likely to be earned.

Candidate B has a fair knowledge of the subject but is not good at answering questions, often not knowing what is required. It is important to understand the different skills (i.e. application, analysis and evaluation) that this paper requires and to appreciate when they are needed. This skill needs a lot of practice and it is doubtful whether candidate B has understood the skill requirements properly or has practised answering past papers. This script would be worth a grade D/E overall.